3 0%

D0407794

IF

WORKING WONDERS

WORKING WONDERS

*The success story of wives engaged in
professional work part-time*

by

PAT WILLIAMS

based on material compiled and edited
by Joan Wheeler-Bennett, Zoe Hersov,
Beatrice Musgrave and Tessa Smith

HODDER AND STOUGHTON

Printed in Great Britain for Hodder and Stoughton Limited, St. Paul's House, Warwick Lane, London, E.C.4 by Northumberland Press Limited, Gateshead

'Is there no way for men to be, but women
Must be half-workers?'

Cymbeline, II.V.I.

'If (they) really want to employ part-time
women, I do not see any practical difficulties. It is a matter of will.

Answer in WISC Questionnaire No. 106

CONTENTS

ACKNOWLEDGMENTS

We are indebted to many people for their support and encouragement through the prolonged business of fact-gathering, assembling and analysis. Chief among them are the 250 busy women who spent their time and thought in answering the long questionnaire. Their intention was to benefit their fellows: we trust that we shall have met our obligation to them by realising their objective.

We are particularly grateful to Miss Irene Hilton and her colleagues of the Women's Employment Federation, a charitable, long established organisation devoted to the career opportunities of girls and women. They allowed us free use of their offices and enhanced our confidence in the usefulness of our project.

We could not have managed without the benevolent dispositions of our husbands and the generous technical assistance of Nancy Maitland and Judy Thomas.

J.W.-B.
Z.H.
B.M.
T.S.

Part One

I

THE BACKGROUND

Four years ago, a small group of married women, all graduates in their thirties, produced a pamphlet called 'Comeback', which they sub-titled 'A Guide to the Educated
Woman Returning to Work'. It was a directory to about
ninety professions, and it was aimed at women with some
qualifications who wished to return to work. It indicated,
through tabulated, Consumer-Guide-like comments, the
prospects each profession offered women, both for full and
part-time work. It also included an introductory essay,
and a page offering useful addresses. In all, it was thirty-two
pages long.

The press comment and public interest attending 'Comeback's' publication, however, was out of all proportion to
its length, and surprised even the women who had produced it. At that time it was the first survey of its kind, and
clearly it lit a small flare in a large, empty area of need,
particularly helpful to those women qualified but in the
dark about the working world they had left and now wanted
to re-enter. Its popularity indicated the necessity for further
study and effective action. A member of the group commented:

'Our survey had no commercial backing or sponsorship,
but at the time it was the first practical guide to the potential returner. It showed a great need for practical and moral
stimulus for women wanting to return to professional
life.'

A few months later, four women drawn from the original
team decided to take 'Comeback's' investigations further,
into a larger and more detailed study. They again decided to
restrict their researches to qualified women, because they

thought they could make a more convincing case for avoiding wastage of skills when those skills had cost time and money to acquire.

They decided, also, to study only women working less than full-time, perhaps with unorthodox hours. 'Comeback' had indicated that the greatest difficulty faced by graduate women returning to work was the need to make some sort of flexible arrangement that would tie in with the constantly varying demands of home and family. Many studies and reports had followed up the initial researches of 'Comeback' in the intervening years, but none had looked at the specific difficulties of part-time work.

The group was interested in the details of how the women arranged their working lives, and whether, financially, they considered working worth it. They knew this would be useful information, hopefully to potential employers often ignorant of the woman's point of view. Mature women, if they have not been working for some time, are usually quite surprisingly isolated from the information they need. The women they meet during the day tend to be others also at home. There is little opportunity for them to discover the remarkable degree of flexible arrangements that women returning to work have made. In fact, those who have returned to work under such flexible arrangements are usually unaware that their case is not necessarily special: they tend to think that their own arrangements are uniquely their own solution.

Again, morale may be low. The women in this survey have all overcome their misgivings about returning to a working world. But in qualified professions an absence of a number of years may mean a subtly altered working environment: colleagues with more experience, promoted perhaps and higher in status, may seem disturbingly competent to a woman who has been 'out of it'. One novelist who answered a questionnaire in this survey enclosed a letter with her replies, in which she speculated about the difficulties of returning to work:

'I know a number of women of my own age who haven't worked while their families were growing up, either because it was impossible or because they thought it unfair to, who now say they would like to have a job. They say this, and I'm sure they mean it, but when asked why they don't, they produce all the obvious domestic difficulties which other women have overcome. Part of them is, in fact, *against* the idea of going out and getting a job. It's not laziness, not even fear that they won't be able to compete, but something more, I think—a kind of paralysis of will. I think that if you've not worked for years—and a lot of women, after all, come straight from university, work for a couple of years and then do nothing for the next twenty or so but run a house and raise babies—you need to be able to make a tremendous effort to go out and engage in what is, after all, a quite different order of life.

'In a sense, a domestic existence, while it can be hard work sometimes, is terribly *easy*: you have no one in authority over you, no timetable that you haven't imposed on yourself, no ways of thinking that are quite different from yours. You may have been bored, frustrated, feel you are nothing but a pair of hands peeling potatoes, and that your mind has atrophied, but you have been *sheltered* to what is, really, a quite incredible extent. As a result, I think a lot of women suffer from a sort of mild agoraphobia, so mild it's barely noticeable.

'This isn't true, of course, of women who've worked steadily throughout the years their children were growing up . . .'

What has emerged from this study has been just this: that those women who somehow kept in touch with their colleagues or their previous jobs—and they form the largest proportion of the survey—have found the least difficulty in returning to work again part-time. One woman, a psychiatrist, reports that she had applied formally for a number of jobs, and was not even short-listed; her present position is the consequence of her work being 'known' by a colleague, and a place created for her in the hospital where she now works.

At the start, this survey was to be statistical and appropriately scholarly. But the group soon realised that they were not equipped, in terms of time, staff or money, to handle so rigidly formal a project, and that, in any case, the incoming material was lively and individual, and a descriptive study would be compensatingly interesting: perhaps, in its unprocessed details, even of greater use. The key, after all, was to be individual attitudes to work, and personal solutions. This is why, in the chapters that follow, so much material is quoted directly from the questionnaires, and may seem repetitive: research material in its raw state can be illuminating, if allowed to stand alone; more telling, in some cases, than statistics or judgments. The range of individual possibility, as well as the overlap in similar circumstances, is more clearly understood by reading such unprocessed material.

By now it is a truism that individual stories come alive in the imagination where generalised summations do not. Another truism is that undramatic success stories seldom make news. This may be why we have heard so little of these successful adjustments. Even the women themselves have been unaware that their individual cases may be interesting, or that there are sufficient like them to indicate a definite pattern of successful part-time work.

The four women who undertook this survey are more or less typical of the 250 others whose working circumstances they investigated. All are in their thirties (as is the largest proportion of the survey), all have children (thirteen between them, and three born during the time they were working on this report), and all are professionals: a systems analyst, researcher, publisher's editor, and social worker. Their husbands work as banker, advertising copywriter, psychiatrist and solicitor. This is very much the flavour of the survey—still-young women, middle-class, comfortable, two interesting professions in the family. Clearly these are families where there is good reason for returning to society the fruit of skill, training, and life experience.

For two years the team of four women worked on the survey on the same irregular part-time basis as the women they were investigating—carrying on with their own jobs, running their homes, dealing with domestic emergencies, overseeing the children, cutting down during school holidays, and adjusting their timetables to accommodate all these varying demands.

In the early stages of writing up the material some time was spent in discussing what word might be used for this 'irregular part-time' working style. The phrase the team had been using, 'less than full-time', was cumbersome—but crucial. Although in the end the perfect word was not found, the clarifying discussion is worth setting down here.

The group had begun by investigating 'part-time' work, but had found this description unsuitable: it implied a regularity and similarity of hours which didn't obtain in their sample. 'Part-time' could mean as much as forty hours a week, as in nursing, or as little as one hour, as in lecturing. The phrase sought without success was one which should somehow indicate this—and indicate, too, that 'less than full-time' can be a permanent arrangement, not an untidy interim phase between two bouts of full-time work.

For women in this survey *like* working 'less than full-time'. As far as they are concerned, it suits their way of life, and they don't want to alter it. The group consider that this point emerged as their most important generalised finding. If their results indicate any more general pattern or trend, then it is this: unorthodox working hours are not a temporary phase, reluctantly adopted (as the assumption has always been) during the child-bearing years, to be dropped later with relief, in exchange for a regular eight-hour daily job.

By the time that domestic responsibilities lessen, most working women have made commitments in the community, with friends and with relatives, which make reasonable and real demands on their time and interest. Their own lives— and presumably the lives of the people they are in contact with—would be thinner and more circumscribed without them. Such commitments are things which a mature adult will not relinquish lightly. Something else arises here as well: a mature woman has the kind of knowledge which can not be formalised in text books or policy statements, but which is as useful to society as any other kind of know-how—except that this cannot really be taught, only gained from experience and exemplified when gained. A social worker in the survey, for instance, wrote:

'My previous employer uses part-timers. But there were no openings when I applied. But in any case, I was not keen to return there. I wanted to be more involved in community development and to put into practice theories evolved, and understandings arrived at, whilst bringing up children.'

The women in this survey quite clearly don't want to make a choice between 'work' and 'home' at the expense of either. To them such a choice is artificial. They quarrel with the sort of conclusion drawn in an *Observer* article early in 1968, marking the fiftieth anniversary of woman suffrage. In it, Ronald Bryden based a comment on the fact that of eighteen million British women of working age, less than 9,000,000 were employed whole or part-time, 61,000 were temporarily out of work, and the remaining nine million were, in the words of the Central Statistical Office, 'economically inactive'. He wrote: 'Half of the women of Britain have accepted the feminist revolution. The other half have rejected it.'[1]

This sort of either/or conclusion, in their opinion, misses the point. First of all, few women (barring professional intellectuals) are given to making such rigid theories about the way they lead their lives. Secondly, this type of artificial choice was sounding a false note even thirty years ago. In 1936 Ray Strachey wrote:

'The feminists of the two decades before the war saw the

problem of employment in an artificial and propagandist light. They thought of work as a satisfaction of personal needs, an outlet for gifts and powers, a fulfilment of personal individuality . . . no doubt an inevitable reaction from the assumptions of middle-class life during the nineteenth century. It was from a really paralysing position that the feminist ideal swung off to the other extreme, and idealised work as if it were the one good thing in life. All the practical facts which tended to upset this point of view were ignored.'[2]

This was the era when a career had, for many women, almost the force of a political or religious 'movement', and to their careers were sacrificed those many aspects of their personalities which would have made them more rounded individuals and more attractive women. The period in which a too clever, too successful career woman seemed formidable and finally pathetic, because so unfeminine—has only recently gone. Then femininity began to be equated in the popular image with frills and little-girl women.

The women in this survey belong to neither extreme. They want a multi-faceted life, and make the point over and over again that each different activity 'feeds' them with stimulus and interest. They are doing what they find is possible, discovering how best to manage. And from the comments of their husbands it turns out that what is possible for these women is a working activity, both domestic and professional, of such wide and energetic proportions that few men would dream of undertaking the equivalent—certainly not at present rates of pay. The picture built up in the questionnaires is of extremely busy, often humorous, adaptable women, fast on their feet, somehow dovetailing the many different demands on them, and happy with their way of life.

Just how difficult this life can be is well summed up by the bursar of a famous school whose doctor wife filled in a questionnaire. He answered in his own words the question enquiring about the husband's attitude to his wife's work, and clearly summarises the essential picture that emerges in the survey:

'In principle,' he writes, 'I strongly support her wish to carry on her profession. If she did not, she would not be so happy a person—and, probably, neither should I!

'In practice she works too many hours in the week (largely because suitable part-time jobs are not available) and too many weeks in the year. This, coupled with looking after a husband, four children, the nannie, the domestics, and so on, means that she hardly ever relaxes for long at home.

'Her hours and her holidays are not unreasonable, but regular hours are very restricting, and flexibility is ideally desirable.'

The points he makes will be re-iterated throughout this book: the personal pleasure that work brings, which reflects back into the family; and the price paid—an arduous working week, requiring the utmost flexibility.

In fact, the extent to which the women in this survey are managing to work satisfactorily in their professions and in their homes is in most cases directly dependent on flexibility. At the heart of it lies their own adaptability coupled with the degree of flexibility they can find in those with whom they have contact—schools, shops, domestic helpers and employers. If a nursery school will agree to take a child for sessions that are not rigidly time-fixed; if a shop stays open until seven p.m.; if a daily woman is prepared to adjust her hours when asked, and if the employer will understand in return for reliable and punctual service that there are unavoidable moments of domestic crisis, then the woman can give of her best both at work and at home.

It is the successful combination of the different strands of their lives that makes many of the women in this survey able to give generously of their professional skills. As the shortage of qualified women becomes more keenly felt in the professions, this will no doubt occur even more widely. F.le Gros Clark observed in a study entitled *Women, Work and Age*:

'... It must be obvious that a nation can only secure the maximum participation of its women on their own terms . . . They are conscious that a contented domesticity is, after all, at the heart of a good life, and that they alone possess most of the arts of managing it.'[3]

To a great extent, the women in this book will speak for themselves. They may be surprised to find themselves in the company of so many others who are also 'coping'. As Dorothy Hodgkin has said:

'This is an experimental age. Almost all young women get married nowadays, and have husbands and families and jobs. So we are all trying to develop patterns that will make this happy as well as possible . . . I think there are almost as many solutions as there are people.'[4]

2

FACTS AND FIGURES

There is no official figure for the number of women engaged in 'less than full-time' work in Great Britain.

Moreover, this particular survey—of 250 women engaged in skilled professional activity—does not claim to be in any sense statistical or scientific. On the other hand, the research team was careful to see that no important occupation in which women do professional work was overlooked.

They sent out 500 questionnaires, of which half were returned. They aimed at a distribution of occupation roughly proportionate to the numbers of women involved in them.

Who they are and what they do

The majority of women in the survey are in jobs which are, in current terminology, service occupations. Teaching leads (70 women, of whom 20 have changed profession), followed by medicine (39, mostly general practitioners). Then comes social work (29, which includes medical and psychiatric).

Twelve women are engaged in some kind of editorial work.

There are four or five women in each of the following professions: broadcasting, business management, architecture, diatetics, university lecturing, psychotherapy, librarianship, computer programming and journalism.

One, two or three women are one of the following: accountant, antiquarian, art historian, artist, biostatistician, child care officer, civil servant, copywriter, dentist, designer, economist, historical researcher, housing manager, laboratory technician, lawyer, market researcher, merchandising consultant, midwife and nurse, musician, novelist, occupational therapist, orthoptist, optician, photographer, physiotherapist, probation officer, psychologist, publisher, radiographer, researcher, social psychologist, speech therapist, statistician, welfare administrator and writer.

Most of the women (168) are married to professional men. The husbands of seventy-four of them are in business of some kind. Three women are widowed, four divorced, and five separated from their husbands.

AMONG THE 250 IN THE GROUP:

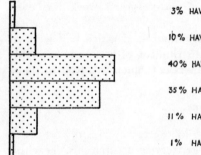

3% HAVE NO CHILDREN	-
10% HAVE ONE CHILD	
40% HAVE 2 CHILDREN	
35% HAVE 3 CHILDREN	
11% HAVE 4 CHILDREN	
1% HAVE 5 CHILDREN	

AMONG THE 250 WOMEN IN THE GROUP
244 HAVE CHILDREN.
TOTAL NUMBER OF CHILDREN IS 617, OF WHOM:

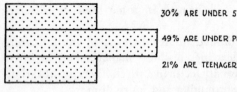
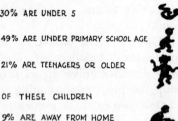

30% ARE UNDER 5

49% ARE UNDER PRIMARY SCHOOL AGE

21% ARE TEENAGERS OR OLDER

OF THESE CHILDREN

9% ARE AWAY FROM HOME

Among them they have 617 children, 180 (nearly one third) of whom are under five. Just under half are of primary school age; 130 are teenagers, and 50 of these are away from home.

They live and work chiefly in London and the Home Counties. A small proportion live in other cities or county towns, north and south from Edinburgh to Cornwall.

The largest number of women in the group are between thirty and forty, followed by a sizeable proportion in the forty to fifty category. A smaller number is either younger or older.

OF THE 250 WOMEN IN THE GROUP:

4% ARE IN THEIR 20s

59% ARE IN THEIR 30s

31% ARE IN THEIR 40s

5% ARE IN THEIR 50s

1% ARE OVER 60

(It is likely that the new formula for working is being established largely by women in their thirties, who were at university after the last war. If there is anything that can be called a trend—a word to be used with discretion—it is that these women have a different attitude to their professional lives from the generation before them, that is women graduates who worked before the war. This is well illustrated by an anecdote quoted by Dorothy Hodgkin in *The Observer*.

'When I decided to get married,' she writes, 'I was already ... a Fellow and Tutor at Somerville. I had to ask formally for permission to marry—this was routine for men and women dons at Oxford. And Miss Darbishire ... said to me:

"Of course you should continue as a Fellow after your marriage, Dorothy, but in my generation, you know, we made a *choice*." [5] Dorothy Hodgkin has, in fact, always worked full-time, and her solution seems to have exemplified the pattern of the generation of graduates previous to the one discussed in this survey. For the generation before her, it was a question of either/or; for her generation 'why not both?', and for the present one, 'both, but only if the work can be managed in a way that suits my life, and in hours that suit my life'.)

The vast majority hold a degree or diploma. Ninety-seven —nearly two-fifths—have more than one qualification. This is, in fact, a very experienced group, a group in which much public and private money has been invested.

A third have undertaken further retraining in connection with their return to work. (See Appendix I.) Of these, twenty had full-time further training. Some paid for it themselves.

One quarter have changed careers—on the whole because suitable work was not available, on their return, in their original occupations; some because their interests changed as they matured.

Interruptions in career have been axiomatic. Ninety-two retired briefly only, when children were born and for short periods after; their comments make it clear that in many cases this was imposed by a fear of losing touch rather than from choice.

Thirty-two retired for 1-5 years. Fifty-three (a quarter) retired for 6-10 years. Twenty-seven retired for 11-15 or more years.

The length of time in retirement seems to have depended on individual circumstances and temperament rather than on the type of work done.

Thirty-two did not retire at all. (Certain professions, it must be remembered, such as writing, reading for publishers and accountancy, for example, can be done at home.)

When they work

One cannot be neat and specific as to when they work. In fact the wide variety in timetables should be an eye-opener to many employers—in particular because the variations are not typical of any one type of profession, but occur across the whole spread of activities.

Most of the sample describe their timetable as 'adaptable at notice'—given warning from work, they can make arrangements at home; given warning that they will be needed at home, they can make arrangements at work.

A very small proportion have to contend with a rigid timetable. They find this extremely difficult and obviously wish it could be otherwise.

Most of the sample consider that they work less than half-time. A smaller proportion work half-time, or more.

The highest proportion work a five-day week but the range is wide during any day: varying from three to nine hours. (In some professions, such as nursing and general practice, even a 40-hour week is considered part-time.)

A smaller but still significant proportion work a four-day week—again between three and nine hours.

If they work, as the smallest number do, a three-day week, then it can again be anything from three to nine hours a day. A two-day or one-day week is usually six or seven hours each day.

Those who work at home, and a few others, describe their hours as 'any time of the day'.

The total of working hours per week ranges from one hour to over forty. The greatest number fall into the 11-20 hour range. Occupations connected with medicine dominate the upper range. Teachers and university lecturers are often in the lower range: but in these cases they have not taken account of the time spent on preparation and correction.

Holiday time is important. Most of the sample arrange to have more holiday time than their male colleagues would expect: 6-8 weeks, paid or (more often) unpaid. Nearly as many make do with 3-4 weeks, and say they would prefer more. The teaching profession comes off best—12-14 weeks, and at exactly the time they need it, when the children are on holiday too. Some have 16-20 weeks (mostly self-employed). A few have only two weeks. And a few say they have no holidays (these were general practitioners).

What they earn is a separate story, covered in Chapter 4.

Most of the women made no plans to stop or start work again at fixed moments. They played it by ear, saw what was possible at any given time, made no manifestos. This may be another difference from an older generation. A graduate in her sixties, invited to comment on this project, remarked: 'Surely such things are thrashed out absolutely clearly by a girl and her prospective husband *before* they marry? How many children they will have, how their joint incomes will be disbursed, how and in what way she will continue her career? That is the intelligent thing to do, you know.'

It seems that both the decision to interrupt the career and to return to it were far less clearly formulated than that. For the women who answered the questionnaire the intention or desire to work was always there, as well as the wish to use training and skills, to widen their own scope of activity and human contact, and to give back to society the training and teaching it had given them. The factors that determined the choice to return to work at one moment rather than another were, as one would expect, more arbitrary: opportunities that arose at the right time, chances that could be taken. This may seem too obvious a point to make much of, but it is worth remembering, simply because when groups or bodies legislate for increasing opportunities, they forget the significance of such small, apparently chance details. The reason, for instance, an advertising copywriter gave for returning to work: 'When my baby was born, I found a flat almost opposite the advertising agency. It was quite by chance.' A domiciliary midwife could work again 'because a new Council Nursery was opened near my home.' Other reasons given were 'a husband retiring' or 'a room suddenly becoming free so that we could have resident help' or 'meeting a former employer'.

A G.P., in her thirties, wrote: 'My sons had become old enough for boarding school. I was known by some of the local medical consultants who actually approached *me* about doing a cytology course, with a view to employing me if all went well. I had been wondering for twelve months just how to pick up the threads of my past career, and this gave me the necessary boost.'

Answers like these, and there are many of them, show life on the move, reservoirs of energy tapped and used: for instance the case where the deliberate co-operation of the employers made work possible for one of their social workers. 'They were my first employers, and after I had returned to work they arranged for me to work on a "term-time only" basis until my children were old enough to be left more easily. Without this transition period, I should have found the return to work much more difficult.'

Sometimes it is a fortuitous event, like the promotion of a husband, that enables a wife to afford the car that can get her to work. Surprisingly often, luck is given as the reason. In all cases, the link in the chain of circumstance extends into the lives and activities of other people, as in that of a woman doctor who found that the wife of a member of the staff (they were living in hospital grounds) was willing to take care of her small child.

This kind of thing cannot be legislated for. One must be alive to the fact that an improvement in one person's circumstances (as in the case of the husband), or in the circumstances of the area (as in the case of the nursery school), will mean an alteration —and often an improvement—in the quality of lives apparently not even directly connected. Factors that played a decisive part in enabling one woman to return to work were:

'A tolerant husband! And as the immediate factor, a good nanny. And then, in the past, an offer of a training by the Americans, who trained me in genetics. These were research methods which, as it happens, I could never have done in this country as a woman G.P.'

Facilities that relieve a woman of some of her domestic commitments are vital links in the chain. Chief among these is suitable domestic help.

Only twelve per cent of the sample manage without any domestic help at all, including a handful who cite the unpaid help of husbands, grandmothers, in-laws, friends and neighbours: co-operative solutions to domestic assistance seem rare. About a third employ paid help more than eight hours a week (and therefore incur tax and insurance costs). Twenty-five per cent employ paid help for less than eight hours a week. Thirty-five per cent have resident help, including au pair girls (who are not full-time).

A number of women have invested part of their earned income in mechanical help: dishwashers, washing machines, motor cars, and so on. Adequate nursery schooling nearby and the use of a car are also important.

But the chief factor which has enabled these women to work again is their children growing up.

3

THREE PROFILES AND A MAP
OF ONE DAY

Now to restore the picture of these proportions and percentages into recognisable human form. Below, we offer three histories as they emerge from the questionnaires, and the map of the day of a fourth woman. These women are not typical: indeed, right through the survey, no particular 'type' emerges. These stories have been chosen because the writers are extremely successful in their part-time fields, and because their replies give an unusually vivid picture of their lives.

MRS. A.

Mrs. A. sets standards for herself which are probably unusually high. She gives a description of a many-sided working week, and makes it clear how she has been drawn into a broader sphere of activities than the domestic or purely working environment. This is true of many women by the time they reach their late thirties. They have commitments —often not easy to label—which have grown organically, and which full-time work would inevitably restrict.

Mrs. A. also makes points, to be raised again and again, about the lack of status for part-timers and the lack of realistic financial return for the work—though she, in fact, does not need to work for the money.

How they returned

Mrs. A. is a psychiatrist specialising in psycho-therapy. She has worked previously in general medicine, pediatrics, and general practice. She qualified fifteen years ago, has postgraduate qualifications in psychiatry, and special training in psycho-therapy and group analytic training. She is married, has two children of six-and-a-half and nearly four, and is 'between thirty and forty' years old. Her husband is a consultant at a London teaching hospital.

Mrs. A. works about twenty-four hours a week, for forty-six weeks in the year, usually between 9.30 a.m. and 4.00 p.m., plus evening lectures and committees. Some of her work is done at home, some at a London teaching hospital, some in various committee rooms, some in Wimpole Street consulting rooms. She describes her timetable as 'adaptable at notice'.

When the complement of domestic help is full she has a young mother's help, a daily help, and occasional help with the cooking, if visitors are coming. 'But usually,' she says, 'the complement is *not* full!'

She filled in some of the details of her working life. This arose from her comment that in fact it was difficult to describe her hours of work, as they varied enormously:

'Basically, my N.H.S. appointment is for three half-days, theoretically ten-and-a-half hours, at a London hospital. But this always extends to approximately fourteen hours.

'In addition, I work with a group of doctors on a research project, which occupies me about two-and-a-half hours each week. None of us is paid for this. Then there are the occasional weeks when many extra hours may be put in, and I find this very rewarding in terms of my clinical work.

'Besides this, my hospital appointment requires me to participate in the teaching of undergraduates and postgraduate students; this includes lectures and seminars on days when I would not otherwise be at the hospital. I enjoy the teaching enormously, but it always involves many, many hours of preparation. The payment, by tradition, is in the form of an "honorarium". The time spent on this, and on preparation for case conferences, is the same for full or part-time staff, and I find that in fact I spend relatively longer — partly, I think, because I have the feeling that I should make better use of the time I have at home than on purely domestic chores. (I exclude, of course, the times when I am needed by the children!)

'I find that I tend to push myself to the maximum use of my resources, to make up for the feeling of being "only a woman" or "only a part-timer"—the latter more than the former.

'Besides all this, I have turned out to be a very popular lecturer to intelligent non-medical audiences, on a variety of psychiatric topics. Students of all subjects particularly value my approach, and I seem to have a flair for promoting frank and helpful discussions. Consequently, I am much in demand among students of non-medical faculties, marriage guidance counsellors, medical social workers, teachers, and so on—and less professional bodies as well, such as P.T.A.s. I don't accept all such invitations—it depends on my sense of committal, and my interest in the body or faculty that invites me. I usually confine these lectures to Oxford, Cambridge and London: and they are paid on an honorarium basis.

'As a lecture is usually arranged several months ahead, I can never predict my domestic help situation at the time, and this can sometimes be a considerable problem. (On the other hand, last March there was an International Colloquium at Cambridge, lasting a week. I was approached two weeks before to lecture in the place of a doctor who was ill. Writing a completely new lecture, on a pre-arranged topic, in a fortnight, and fitting in two trips to Cambridge, was a considerable challenge, which at first I was reluctant to accept. In the end, the result was well worth the effort, and somehow or other home, hospital work, and the children, kept ticking over quite normally. Looking back, I am still wondering how!

'The point is that all sorts of extras come one's way—in as large a volume as if one were full-time.

'Because of my knowledge of psychiatry (and child psychiatry) and an interest in education, I have been talked into being Chairman of P.T.A. of my son's school. Because of my very cordial relationship with all the staff of the school, I am sometimes consulted professionally. Is this unpaid work or voluntary community service? I find that because I am both a mother and a professional woman I am especially well-placed to understand problems regarding schools—and very readily available for such consultation!'

Mrs. A. interrupted her career for five years, during which time she did a little unpaid teaching and work for marriage guidance counsellors. When she wanted to return to work she was invited to apply for the post she now holds—as it happened, the senior consultant psychiatrist at the hospital for which she now works was a consultant during her period as registrar at another hospital. 'Efforts to find work were fruitless with people not familiar with my work ability: I was never short-listed. Approaches to people who knew me and what I could do resulted in an effort to persuade a committee to create a new position!'

She finds that both in psychotherapy and child psychiatry part-time workers are usual and accepted, although most institutions like more sessions than she can manage to give. Psychiatry itself is 'on the verge' of accepting part-timers: 'Part-time workers are just beginning to appear here and there, as departments feel the pinch for good staff.'

It is one of the themes of all these questionnaires that even though part-timers may be grudgingly admitted into their fields of work, the employer is, at the same time, gaining by their part-time work. Mrs. A. was asked if her employer 'gained' in some way, and her reply was vehement: 'And how! I put in lots of extra hours. Also, the hospital is my major professional committal—I don't share it with private practice or another hospital.'

Her colleagues, too, are co-operative and helpful, understanding if she has to change a lecture to suit domestic needs.

In her particular circumstances, she finds her difficulties are few, mostly 'nuisance value'. She doesn't think she has any income left after she has paid expenses—'but then I rely on my husband for income!' Lack of domestic help can be a strain, 'but mostly I have enough.' Distance from work is 'a nuisance, that's all.' Another nuisance is 'the need to work late on one day at least, because of the difficulties of some patients in getting time off from work. Thanks to a very co-operative husband, I work late on a day he can usually be home by 5.30, should the domestic help situation require it.'

She is enthusiastic about the help and support she gets from her husband, and his consistent encouragement. But, 'like most husbands, he does not realise how stretched I am when I try to work with inadequate domestic help!' And, not surprisingly on the facts as given—'he says I take on too much!'

Then she adds the salient point with which all women in this survey would probably agree: 'But what is not too much under ideal conditions becomes so when one is short of help or when, for example, the children are ill.'

She manages to spend a lot of time with her children— time, she makes clear, when she is positively 'there', not merely physically under the same roof. 'They accept my working,' she says, 'and value the time I spend with them. The little one reverted to thumb-sucking when I returned to work. It has passed. Both, of course, appreciate the status I have with the school! I am at home by 4.00, and earlier on Tuesdays and Fridays. Weekends are spent with them.

'But really my children find what I do part and parcel of living—the life they have always known. After all, lots of women are out a lot although they don't work—even just "going shopping!"—and I don't do that unless I absolutely have to. I gave my time to my children almost completely when they were very small—and since then I have, so far, been lucky in having good, pleasant girls to leave them with.'

Mrs. A. makes a final point, which is often repeated else-where, about the difficulty of promotion in part-time posts.

Within her own profession she suggests ways of making the best possible use of trained professional part-time women: 'Make more part-time posts, with permanency or possibilities of promotion built into the structure.' But even so, she herself has no intention of returning to full-time work: 'I am extremely lucky. I have a helpful husband and enough money to pay for domestic help—and lots of it—when it is available! I was very active, and on a committee related to my work, just before I went back to work again, and I am sure that the renewal of old contacts helped here. But as for full-time work . . . It was a sweat without children anyway. And it certainly wouldn't be fair to the children now.'

MRS. B.

Mrs. B. is a well-known journalist. Her previous professions have been youth leader, researcher and scriptwriter for documentary films. She has a history honours degree, is between forty and fifty, and is married, with a girl of fifteen and a boy of thirteen. Her husband is the managing director of a private company.

She works variable hours—'between seven and thirty a week, depending on the time of year,' for forty weeks of the year—'roughly coinciding with school terms.' Her work is done mostly in the mornings plus two or three afternoons when very busy. It is done, on the whole, at home.

She has two 'daily women' to help her. Between them they work seven to thirteen hours a week. Before Easter 1966, however, she had help from a 'daily woman' working from 9.00 a.m. till 3.00 p.m.

Until three or four years ago Mrs. B. worked 'rather more than half-time,' and 'had some money left out of my earnings,' once working expenses were paid. (She is paid on a retainer fee from her paper, which doesn't vary according to the amount of work done.) Now, however, her time and pay have been cut—'with both children at a grammar school I found they needed me at home by 4.30 p.m. to help settle them down to homework. But in any case, I was not so much "making money" as having an interest that "pays off".'

While Mrs. A.'s emphasis was on her social commitments, Mrs. B.'s is on her children. She describes at length how her working life has been tailored to their needs—'I *could* earn a great deal more money if I worked full-time. But this would mean neglecting the children, since no paid help can deal with their requests for information on school subjects, human relationships, or sex, for instance. I'm sure some-one else could answer my children's queries as well as I do, but where could you find someone with a similar sympathetic approach to children available every day from 4.30 p.m. and during school holidays?'

Children make different demands at different stages of development, and most mothers in this survey adjust their working lives to accommodate this fact, as Mrs. B. has done:

'For example, my children wanted to come home to lunch each day when they first went to infant school, and they wanted to see me, and have me cook for them. During their last year or so at junior school they wanted to stay for school lunch, to play with friends. They came in for tea, and dashed out again to play with friends. Consequently, I had a great deal of time free.

'Once they started grammar school both wanted to see me at the end of the school day. Neither had done any home-work while at junior school. The new school atmosphere, the emphasis on academic work, the need to make new friends, to get to know several members of staff instead of one form mistress or master, and the more formal work, made them both tired and uncertain. Neither knew how to work at something which didn't interest them, and they needed someone to encourage them to learn self-discipline about getting their homework done. The "learning" habit is not easily acquired, and although I had paid help, prepared to give my children affection and food at the end of the school day, if I was out "homework" was not her responsibility. It became clear to me that if my children were to be as happy and absorbed by school as they had been in a creative junior school, then I had to help them to use their "academic" ability and help them find outlets in the home for their frustrated "creative" ability.

'Both now know how to work and neither ever complains of nothing to do. In many ways this means more effort on my part but has given me, in the end, more free time. Similarly, the fact that I was nearly always prepared to cook "favourite" dishes and thoroughly enjoyed cooking has probably encouraged them to cook for themselves.'

Mrs. B. is one of the people in the survey who has changed profession because of family responsibilities:

'If I had not married I would have continued to work in films. But going away on location made it difficult to get to know my husband, and as soon as this became clear to me I willingly abandoned this interesting career.'

Then she changed careers again: 'When I had children I had to find work I could do at home. Neither my husband nor my children are demanding. But they all need care and affection, and I enjoy being married and bringing the children up with my husband. Before I had satisfactory personal relationships my work came first. I had ten years of full-time work before I had children. The work was my priority. Now my family comes first and until the children leave home I shall put their needs before the demands of a job.'

But in any case her employer makes marginal gains, she feels, by employing her part-time: 'I have a great deal of knowledge, experience, and it is known that I am always available (by telephone if not in person) for consultation about contacts, educational problems and so on.'

She was asked about 'special difficulties', and once again her children lay at the heart of her answer as she voiced a difficulty experienced by many mothers in this survey:

'I now for the first time for seventeen years do not have adequate daily help. This is not by choice, but because I

cannot obtain help of this kind. I have always had someone
who put my children before the housework. Consequently,
when the children had mild illnesses I could leave them,
when necessary, with an easy conscience. Now they are
older I do not care for them to come into a large, empty,
fairly isolated house.

'When the children were younger there was always someone at home (paid domestic willing to stay on) if I was out
when they returned from school.'

Her children, she says, think she is fortunate to have an
interest. But they know they come first. 'They would like
me to do more work—in theory. But, as an example, last
week I was out three evenings running—which is very
unusual—and they were strained and quarrelsome, even
though there was an adult here, and my husband came home
early from work.'

Mrs. B. reports no opposition to women part-timers in
her work, although 'the profession regards all women journalists with suspicion.' She says that the change within the
profession that would make the best possible use of women
part-timers would be greater use of women full-time—'the
profession would perhaps become more sympathetic to
women in general.'

Yet she herself would not wish to return to full-time work.
Her reasons against the idea are the same as the majority
of the women in this survey: 'I have developed many interests locally—voluntary nursery schools, service as a gover-
nor and school manager, which I have no wish to abandon.
Also, there are far too few well-informed men and women
working locally who are prepared to play a part in local
authority schools. I may want *almost* full-time work when
the children leave home.

'Although not ambitious, I had a very successful "career"
prior to marriage. In retrospect I see that I had a series
of most interesting and demanding jobs. None of these had
normal hours, and all made stringent demands on intelligence, health and time. In youth work one had to be available

every evening and much of the programme planning for 2,000 members(many from overseas) had to be done during the daytime. Film work had unusual hours and locations, and one had to learn to co-operate with people with widely varying talents, jobs and interests.

'When I married I found I had to take a less demanding job with normal office hours. But my husband didn't demand this—I believe the marriage did. Similarly when I had children I gave up work, and missed it very much. Indeed, I was bored and lonely, and didn't enjoy household chores.

'I missed intellectual stimulation, the company of colleagues and the demands of a job. I was very fortunate to be approached to do research jobs (on demand only—I didn't think it right to leave my child, although I knew I wanted to escape from "domesticity and the demands of a child"). These occasional jobs kept me cheerful and occupied until my second child was born. Then I was approached by the paper for which I have now worked for thirteen years.

'At times the work has been so exciting and demanding that it came first. It would be difficult to say why I didn't work full-time when I found the work so rewarding. But I knew from my very first piece of research for the paper, on "Juvenile Delinquency", the importance of a mother's role. This knowledge was reinforced by Bowlby's work, and my own personal observation of children's problems in the voluntary nursery school when it was first established in my area.

'There was a conflict between my knowledge (reinforced by my maternal instinct), and my enjoyment of intellectually demanding work. Moreover, I had a guilty feeling about paying back society a debt I felt I owed, since I knew I was one of the few privileged women to have had a university education.

'The conflict has become less acute over the past three or four years.

'In part this is because I enjoy the intellectual demands

my children now make on me. Also I enjoy watching their personalities and interests develop—and so does my husband. Moreover, I know they will soon leave home.

'One knows whether one has done a good piece of work— whether it's organising, administrating or writing—often in all too short a time. With children one can never be certain one has worked well, but as they grow older one can see that all the time, effort and intelligence spent were worth while. Therefore one is prepared to give more readily, and somehow the rewards seem greater.'

So Mrs. B. quite emphatically feels part-time work to be 'a great boon'—'it should be much more widely available. It means that the intelligence and energy of women is available outside the home, but much more important, it means, given flexible hours, that the woman is available to meet the needs of husband and children. During certain years, and unquestionably during the first few years of a child's life, the mother (unless she dislikes children or is a very unsuitable mother) should be available at home.

'What interests me is how one can persuade women that time spent on children is not time wasted. It is a problem which concerns me.

'However, few women could work well at being a wife and mother and part-time professional worker unless given mental and moral support by a loving husband. My husband has never regarded time given to the children or to work outside the home as time stolen from him. His attitude is unusual.'

MRS. C.

Mrs. C. is a lecturer in further education in statistics. Before that she was an administrative civil servant. She has an M.A. (Cantab.) in Economics Parts I and II. She is 'between thirty and forty', married to an administrative civil servant. She employs paid domestic help—twelve hours a week—and lectures an average of nine hours a week (with additional time spent on marking, preparation, etc.) in a thirty-two week working year. She has a boy and a girl, aged six-and-a-half and eight-and-a-half respectively.

Mrs. C.'s emphasis is on the details and difficulties of her job:

'First, it is important that my abilities are in a "shortage speciality", i.e. statistics and economics.

'Shortly after my first child was born I started seeking part-time occupation and put my name down with the local College of Technology for part-time teaching there. Nearly two years later, just after my second child was born, I was asked to take over an evening class in statistics. This was January 1960. I taught in evening classes only until September 1963, when I commenced part-time day classes, and I now teach only daytime students. This last year my students have been:

1. B.Sc. Sociology—Statistical Methods for Part I (external London degree).
2. H.N.D. in Business Studies—Statistical Methods.
3. Professional students in Accountancy—Statistics.

'I am just coming to the end of my third year of part-time (day) teaching at the college. All my students are whole-time (as opposed to day release) on established courses and there is no difference between the work I do and that done by full-time members of staff.

'As a part-time lecturer, I am a casual, paid as such and treated as such and without permanent establishment. Some six months ago I decided to pursue this matter with my Head of Department and Principal of the College. I felt it was time the permanence of my part-time connections with the College were recognised by a proper part-time salary, by integration into the work and organisation of the Department and by my having responsibility for a specific part of the teaching work, instead of a highly diversified responsibility.

'I did not get very far with my attempts. I was assured there would always be part-time teaching for me—my value in a shortage speciality—but on the salary and responsibility point, little was forthcoming. However, I did eventually gain the support of the Principal and despite the initial unfavourable reaction of the Local Education Authority (who are responsible as this is a Regional College of Technology) he promised to pursue my case and to get me established on a part-time salary for September 1966. It was clear that in so doing he was *not* favouring me as a married woman, but trying to ensure that my services were not lost to the College. The Principal knew quite well that he would find it very difficult to replace me.

'However, all this was overtaken by other events! Exasperated by lack of support at the College of Technology I applied for a post (part-time) at another further education establishment within the ambit of the University of London, to lecture in Statistics to Sociology students (B.Sc. [Ext.] Soc. London). This I obtained, on those terms which I had tried, without success, to obtain from my present college. So in September I shall go elsewhere, on an established, salaried, half-time basis.

'After I had obtained this new post, all my requests at the College of Technology would have been met, in order to retain me. Had I met with a more forthcoming attitude initially it is doubtful whether I would ever have applied for a post elsewhere.

'In my view, arrangements such as those under which I have worked, and which do not provide a proper part-time career, are a form of exploitation. Undoubtedly I was looked upon as expendable, and only my personal value in a shortage speciality enabled me, to some extent, to dictate my own terms, e.g. work in mornings only. But in lecturing, where administrative responsibilities are specifically allocated and teaching functions can be exercised on some days of the week only, the scope for part-time staff is very considerable. Many more could be employed, without increasing the burdens of full-time colleagues.'

A MAP OF THE DAY

Mrs. D. has two children (aged twelve and nine), lives in Wimbledon and works as a publisher's production manager and art editor two days a week (Tuesdays and Fridays). She also works at home, averaging another twelve to fifteen hours a week. She has a production assistant to help her with her work one morning a week. She tries to divide her work so that lengthy designing and editorial jobs are done at home, leaving her free to concentrate on the administrative side of her job at the office.

AN OFFICE DAY

7.30 Gets up.

7.45 Breakfast with family, prepared by au pair girl.

8.10 Waves goodbye to small son who catches school bus.

8.15 Drives husband and daughter to station and school respectively, herself to supermarket. Plans menus and shopping list while sitting in car outside supermarket (as she does not like thinking about food late at night). This is the important twice-weekly shopping, which leaves her free for work or other activities on the remaining days.

9.30 Cup of coffee and chat with au pair. Glance at paper. Makes herself a sandwich for the office while au pair unpacks shopping and is briefed about supper preparations. Makes bed, sorts out laundry for washing-machine, and completes make-up and dress for office.

10.15 Leaves by car for South Kensington office. Arrives near office about twenty minutes later and looks for parking space. Carries with her a large bag containing most of her records, as these have to be used both at home and at the office.

10.45 Arrives at office, greets colleagues, checks typewriter has not been removed, dusts desk and empties someone else's ashtray if necessary, begins to sort work which has accumulated in two trays (one for letters and messages, the other for MSS and proofs, block-proofs, art work and less urgent sales literature). Makes notes on action necessary.

11.00 Gets down to concentrated work until about 5.00 p.m. Usually has sandwich lunch at office but some days goes out for a quick pub lunch with colleagues or a little shopping in the vicinity. (Social lunches, shopping expeditions and other sorties are reserved for non-office days.) During the day sorts out muddles and delays, confers with chief and colleagues, sends out specifications for estimating, orders paper and binding materials, etc., corrects jacket and book proofs for typography, marks up art work and corrects blockproofs (ready for next collection by blockmaker), briefs artists and designers and sees printers, binders, blockmakers and other suppliers by appointment. Puts aside lengthy designing, reading and editorial jobs to be done at home later.

Between 5 and 5.30

Walks back to car trying to forget about work. Drives home through rush hour, anything from forty minutes to an hour.

Around 6

Arrives home, greets children and au pair and hears about their day. Asks about homework, checks that cat has been fed and children have stopped eating biscuits. Begins to cook supper while au pair clears up in kitchen and lays table. If home early, snatches cup of coffee or something stronger and another glance at paper. If any telephone messages, tries to fit in calls before husband arrives at station.

6.45 Husband having telephoned from station, drives down to meet him. Brief exchange of news in car, before children make private conversation impossible.

7.00 Supper, unless son asks for extension to watch sports programme, with maybe a quick drink before.

7.45 Helps au pair to clear supper things and wash up; supervises son's music practice and occasionally both children's homework. Sorts out son's clothes for school and sometimes helps with bath, hairwash, etc.

9.00 End of official day.

4

MONEY

'None but a fool will take a wife whose bread must be earned solely by his labor, and who will contribute nothing towards it herself.'
A Present to a Servant Girl, 1743

'My husband encourages me to work, but he says that as far as pay is concerned, it's no more than a subsidised hobby.'
Answer in WISC Questionnaire No. 183

The librarian earns 5s 11d an hour. The psychiatrists and copywriters earn five guineas an hour. But it is clear that at neither end of the scale do the women in this survey work for the money—or rather, for the money alone.

If the man is traditionally the breadwinner—and in this sample he is nearly always a professional man, steadily employed and with a good income—then it is reasonable to assume that the working wife will be providing the cake.

Often she does. ('My earning has meant the difference between having a holiday each year and staying home,' writes a teacher.) On the whole, by the time she has made arrangements for coping with her domestic commitments, paid out more cash for expensive foods which take less time to cook, invested in the machinery—from car to dishwasher—that will cut down time on chores, and paid the extra tax on the joint income, half or less of her salary is usually all that remains.

The old saw still holds true: the British tax system makes it more economic to divorce but to continue to live together, than for married partners to work and pay joint tax.

But first, let us look more closely at what the women in this sample earn. Estimates of pay were asked for on an hourly basis. While some of the women found it difficult to make such estimates accurately, especially where hours of work were indefinite, it is still possible to describe these rates broadly.

Occupations which offer payment of two pounds and over are confined to lecturing (and here the technical colleges are best), specialist medicine, dentistry, computer programming, advertising and psychotherapy.

Conspicuously low rates of pay exist in nursing, social work, library and museum work, all forms of research, including medical, and publishing.

Teaching and general medical practice come off well by comparison—these are professions where equal pay is accepted in principle.

This particular sample of working wives is comfortably off, and only five say they are at work because the family requires the money. (In one of these families the husband is studying for a further degree.) And perhaps because money is not the chief incentive in the majority of cases, most of the women are quite surprisingly vague about how their rates of pay compare with those of men, or with those of full-time colleagues.

A quarter—mostly teachers, doctors, and social workers— think their pay rates are lower than the equivalent full-time rates. A tenth think they are higher. A quarter think they are being paid less than a male counterpart. The majority think their rate of pay appropriate to the work they do. But few seem to have checked up, and few seem to be militantly concerned.

They are far more specific about the startling diminution of their earnings through expenses. The more you earn the less you keep, and the top end of the scale is heavily taxed. About twenty per cent reckon their take-home pay as one quarter or less of their earnings. About thirty per cent expect to take home half their earnings. And less than fifty per cent calculate their take-home pay as three quarters. Some of the women who say they net less than a quarter of their take-home pay are in the most highly skilled professions.

The women speak for themselves:

Journalist: I take home one third of my thirty shillings an hour. What hurts us is the supertax my husband must pay. I would pay at least five pounds a week for help even if I didn't have my job, but I have subtracted it here as if it were an expense created by my job.

Physiotherapist: My expenses are high, and include petrol and car maintenance, extra clothing and stockings, extra food and laundry bills (time-saving), extra money given to children in holidays for tennis, swimming, etc., which occupy them while I am at work.

G.P.: I find that for some of my sessions the woman I employ as mother's help actually gets more than I do when expenses are taken into account.

Editor and reader: I take home half. This makes my net earnings the same as my cleaner's. I reckon her wages as 'expenses'. I pay full 'self-employed rate' National Insurance stamps so that I can get Maternity Allowance, and I also pay Life Insurance premiums as the work I do doesn't provide a pension. If you count these two items in among the expenses, then none of my earnings remain. I am, in fact, running at a loss.

Of the women who keep about three quarters of their income one often finds that work is being done at home. (There are exceptions, like the teacher who bicycles to work to keep down costs.) Travelling and clothes expenses are not needed, nor are marginal expenses which mount up and are repeated over and over again: 'more expensive food, which saves cooking and shopping time.'

Domestic help is extremely expensive, but there is not one complaint about the price of such services (although many women object to the attendant Selective Employment Tax).

The main criticism arises, in fact, over the joint assessment of husband and wife for income tax purposes. Interestingly enough, this was more often made by the many husbands who contributed personally to this survey than by the wives. The husbands straightforwardly condemn the 'iniquities' of the tax system, even as they declare their pride and pleasure at their wives' professional activities in other respects. For even a modest contribution by his wife may put a man who has achieved high professional or managerial rank into the surtax bracket. The resentment that this may cause may well be keeping many highly qualified women away from work.

Several women pointed out that the wife whose earnings are separately assessed for income tax purposes may spare her husband some anguish and, if she can be classed as 'self-employed', may even save herself some money.

Replies were very informative on the tax question:

Freelance writer and broadcaster: Out of £42 10s per month I get £14 10s. My babyminder on the other hand earns over £20 a month. What incentive do I have to use my qualifications and experience?

The basic problem financially is that I pay almost half my income on babyminding facilities and almost the other half on tax payable on my whole income.

Tax relief on payments for domestic help and babyminding costs would solve this problem. Also perhaps relief from the National Insurance and Selective Employment Tax would be a great help.[6]

Doctor: I keep one quarter of £1 per hour. Although this seems a small margin of profit I would probably have similar domestic help even if not working because this is the only way one's children and oneself can have a full life when there are five of them. There should, however, be tax relief for the domestic help required. It should not be necessary to pay Selective Employment Tax for help to enable one to pursue a profession not in itself eligible for Selective Employment Tax.

Dental surgeon: I keep one quarter of £2 2s. I find my general housekeeping expenses quite reasonable for this number of hours. If I increase at all my expenses rise considerably and I lose the feeling of control over every aspect of the house.

Psychoanalyst: I think it is very hard that although there is a great demand for qualified women doctors in every branch of the profession we are not allowed tax exemption for the expensive domestic help we must employ in order to live a useful professional life; nor in further postgraduate training are the heavy fees we pay subject to tax relief.

Among the women in this survey money is seldom the factor that determines their decision to work. This may be a contributing cause as well as the effect of the low rates of pay for women in many professions. The fact that this pay is further diminished by tax and by expenses unavoidably incurred when working outside the home, is considered a definite discouragement, but it is not enough of a disincentive to prevent these women from working.

5

CHILDREN AND DOMESTIC HELP

Children make different demands at different stages of development, and most mothers adjust their working lives to accommodate this fact. From their answers it becomes clear that in a perfect world the working hours of mothers would coincide with the times their children are at school. In most cases this is only a dream. In fact some teachers do come close to realising it. Also, more noticeably than in any of the other professional groups, teachers' children don't mind that their mothers work; sometimes they don't even know. 'They are quite happy,' writes one, 'as long as my work doesn't interfere with their lives, and it very seldom does.' Holidays—which present great difficulty to many of the other women—are no problem either. Another teacher describes her fortunate situation, indicating her own added pleasure in life now that she is working again, and implying that this pleasure has been transmitted to her child:

'My children are quite unaffected. I teach in an independent school, and have excellent holidays. I am always home when they come home. My youngest child, born after I started teaching, seems a particularly contented child. I never feel impatient with him, and really enjoy him.'

The next most relaxed situation for children seems to be the one in which the children have never known a time when their mothers haven't worked—an excellent argument for those intending to return to work to do so quickly. A neuropathologist, mother of nine-year-old twins, writes:

'They've never known anything else. They are quite accepting. And I arrange my day so that I see them and cope with them from 6.30 a.m. to 8.30 a.m., and from 7.30 p.m. to 8.30 p.m.'

And a speech therapist with a six-year-old, a four-year-old, and a two-week-old-baby, says:

'They have accepted the fact that I work on Mondays and Fridays, and that I am not available on these days. They have never known the situation otherwise, as I worked part-time from the moment I was married.'

A psychiatrist found the question of her children's attitude to her work 'irrelevant'. Her children had never known any other situation, and thus it was simply a fact of their lives.

If the mother stops working for more than a few months when her children are born, it seems that the best time to go back to work is when the children are old enough to understand what their mothers do. The majority of mothers in the survey did in fact wait until their children were at primary school, before deciding to return to work. From this age onwards it is easier to involve children in their mother's activity. From the answers it is clear that whenever it is possible for children to see their mother's work or to share it in some way—even if only in terms of anecdotes—their understanding and tolerance are greatly increased. Again, teachers are fortunate here. Many of their children enjoy going to school with their mothers. A nursery school teacher with children aged eight and five works almost exactly the same hours as her children spend at their school. 'But they like to come with me whenever they have the odd day off from school and I still have to go to the nursery.'

When the mother's work ceases to be a rival for attention and grows into a source of interest for the children, everyone benefits, as the quotes show:

General Secretary of a Welfare Society: My elder son is interested, and sometimes helps during holidays with simple jobs in the office.

Doctor: They accept my work happily, and enjoy accompanying me on the occasional visit.

Doctor: They have never known any other arrangement, and accept the situation readily. They are helpful and co-operative, and come to work with me frequently when free to do so.

Social worker: I have tried to involve my children in my work, and the office is seven minutes away from my home and their schools. I always took four to six hours' work away from home, and did regular voluntary social work. They accept it now without any difficulty. I tell them what I'm doing, and how.

Novelist: They obviously get pleasure out of having a parent who writes books, and don't miss any opportunity to boast and show new editions.

Teacher: My children find it interesting except in the holidays. The youngest child comes with me twice a week and this he considers a great treat.

Music teacher: They are very interested and approve of my activities, although it sometimes means they have to get their own meals, especially tea, or wait until I get back. They find it fun that I teach some of their friends and all my pupils are roughly their contemporaries. They certainly approve of the financial side of it.

Housing manager: If they became worried I found it stopped if they were shown where I went and what I did.

With older children, this kind of involvement or interest in their mother's work is often coupled with an absorption in their own pursuits, and a healthy independence:

Psychoanalyst: Now that they are older they both express relief at not having to feel guilty for leading their own lives, as with, in some cases, an unoccupied mother.

Economist: They are both full-time at school, and now do a lot of work themselves, on their own.

The ideal outcome of having an interested, working mother is embodied in the response of this twenty-year-old medical student, son of a medical artist, who filled in the relevant question himself:

'Her work is a very good example to us of hard work and highly efficient organisation in fitting in so much. It helped, in fact, to arouse my interest in medicine.'

And a dietician's daughter wrote: 'Working makes mum a much more interesting person, and easier to live with.'

Responses are so personal that generalisations are hazardous. One mother commented that although theoretically working arrangements were made much easier when the children were older, she herself had found that this was the time when her active, or creative, presence was most necessary. Her daughters, aged sixteen and fifteen, were on the brink of their first independent, near-adult encounters with the outside world, and were nourished by the constant, informal contact with their mother. 'It was much simpler when they were smaller,' she said. 'I had very good domestic help. But they are at the age now when it is *me*, and *my* experience, that they need.'

Each case is different. But the experience of others is often helpful in some ways. A number of mothers make it clear that the children accept their absence from home most easily if there is a constancy and regularity about it. A dental surgeon writes: 'My five-year-old accepts my schedule very well because it is constant week in and week out. I think if I changed my hours at all, particularly if I were not home at bedtime, he would be upset.'

At all ages, and particularly when the children are young, domestic help of some kind is essential for a working mother. Without it, she is bound to the house. Difficulties are considerably lessened if the help is good and of the right kind:

School counsellor: My children accept my work, and enjoy the company of the woman who looks after them.

G.P.: They enjoy the company of a responsible female teenager twice a week during the holidays, and probably she shares some of their interests better than I do. They sometimes ask why I don't go to work more!

Educational psychologist: My youngest child is at nursery school, and doesn't realise that I am at work while she is at school. The odd afternoon is spent quite happily with a beloved mother's help or a friend.

But if the quality of the alternative company is not harmonious, then something must be done:

Teacher: Their response to my work is good. They are interested, and have always been used to my leaving them—for limited periods—with a substitute mother. If anything *does* make them resentful, they say so, and I am warned!

Social worker: They are interested in my work, and somewhat proud. Yet they are resentful at times during school holidays, when they are looked after by their grandmother. This is not an altogether satisfactory solution.

'Ideally,' writes a neuropathologist, in part of a long comment on how domestic help would be best arranged, 'one needs two resident helps. One to take the household off one's back, and one to concentrate on the welfare of the children ... You want an intelligent person to cope with the children, especially during their holidays. But intelligent women do not, by definition, devote themselves to other people's children or households for more than a short time at a stretch. So there is a sword of Damocles always hovering —namely the need to find a replacement.'

In this survey the amount of help employed at home

bears no direct relation to the hours worked by the mother, although the quality of the help is crucial. Much depends on the ages of the children—and many women say they would employ domestic help whether they themselves worked or not. The difficulty of finding suitable domestic help is one of the most commonly identified obstacles in the pursuit of a career, though a small percentage of this sample does manage without.

OF THE 250 WOMEN IN THE GROUP:

34% HAVE RESIDENT DOMESTIC HELP

28% HAVE 8 HOURS' OR MORE HELP PER WEEK

25% HAVE LESS THAN 8 HOURS' HELP PER WEEK

13% HAVE NO DOMESTIC HELP AT ALL

Many sagas arise from dependence on paid help to provide cover for the working mother:

Medical practitioner: I had an excellent daily help for four and a half years who came regularly three mornings a week and to cover me at other times if needed while I worked. Two months ago she unfortunately left her husband and Cambridge.

By great good luck I have found an excellent woman who can at present cover my two regular surgeries but has another job and her timetable is not as flexible as my previous help's who had only me. This limits the amount of extra work (locum, etc.) I am able to do.

I do not like to leave my husband any work except in an emergency as he works very hard.

I use friends only in dire emergencies.

Radio and T.V. interviewer: I am absolutely dependent on

these two people. The mother's help is a foreign girl over here studying for a year. She helps with all domestic chores, and with the children. She has three afternoons and three evenings off. Otherwise she is always here to take charge if I go out. I pay her £5 per week and insurance stamp. My cleaner costs £3 5s a week and can also take charge of the children in my absence. Outlay—approximately £10 per week, before I can go out to work. No tax relief!

Medical practitioner: The daily woman who lives near comes for seventeen hours a week mostly when I am out at work, washes up, cleans the place, including washing some paint at spring cleaning times. Does the ironing. Loves children. (Has five of her own, youngest ten years.) So can cope during school holidays as long as I have precooked the meals. Worth her weight in gold (and knows it) but I still have to do all the thinking.

Another mother puts succinctly the difficulties when reliable domestic help is lacking: 'I could make a better contribution if I felt there was someone on whom I could rely to come and mind the children, so I did not have to be away from work if they are ill—sort of part-time aunt—but of necessity this sort of person would have to be available locally and at short notice, and be acceptable and known to the children, and this is too much to expect. Half-term and other holidays are also a problem. Help with cleaning— if it could be found and if it were reliable—would reduce one's own fatigue, but is not essential.'

In the last decade, however, the number of domestic workers has dropped dramatically. The difficulty of finding them is even greater than that of paying out unrealistic sums from part-time earnings.

. . .

The nursery school or play group can be a boon to the

working mother as well as to her children. Most of the mothers with small children find that they have to rely to a great extent on private or co-operative nursery schools. State nursery schools are virtually non-existent for women who work from choice. And neither type—state or private— is flexible enough about the times of the children's attendance. One mother who requires a nursery school for only three days of the week, finds that those in her area will only take children full-time, 'and won't consider anything less.' Another says: 'A nursery class was opened in this district particularly to provide places for teachers' children, but the hours are useless. I could neither take nor collect my child on the days I worked.'

The rigidity of the schools does make life difficult. A university lecturer says: 'I have been offered many hours' work during the day, which I have been unable to accept because of finding no one to look after the baby.' And she suggests: 'Education authorities should provide nurseries for under-school-age children of teachers. These special nurseries should cope with small babies as well as toddlers, and should be as close to educational establishments as possible.'

The following comment comes from a G.P.: 'I was particularly impressed by the provision made for professional women in the U.S.S.R. Full-time play centres are maintained where women are employed, food shops are open on a skeleton staff until 11 p.m. and consumer goods are available after working hours. Although this may be more difficult in this country I think it is time that we accepted the reality that most women like to keep some professional interest: and in the case of doctors a few hours at a hospital where their children can play together plus easier shopping hours could enable more to work.'

No matter what solutions are found, no matter how good the domestic help or how loving the au pair, whatever the working arrangements may be, emergencies will collapse them, and then the co-operation and patience of everyone concerned is required. The first emergency, of course, is that of the domestic help itself:

Doctor: All my children give me every support they can while I work, but during the last domestic crisis, when the Nanny was leaving, my elder son said: 'Perhaps it would be better if you gave up, Mum.'

The next, constant worry, in which domestic staff is of little help, is that of illness:

Teaching coach: My employer is very ready to accept children's illness as a valid reason for my absence, but my lack of domestic help is a worry in case a child is ill for a longer time or only not quite well. I call on friends and grand-mothers—it is the only thing to do, and I am fortunate in being able to.

Social worker: My salary isn't really enough to employ a living-in mother's help, and at the same time achieve some financial gain . . . But it is absolutely necessary to retain an old age pensioner as a domestic, in order to cater for the children's emergencies.

There is hardly a questionnaire in which the mother does not mention illness as a source of worry and difficulty. Those mothers whose children have been quite well through the period they have worked mention it as an apprehension, and wonder how they will cope if a child does become sick.

Architect: Sickness tends to make them tearful, and if it were ever needed, I would stay automatically. This hasn't happened yet, but I feel sure it will.

Social worker: Leave for children's illness is the most diffi-cult problem and depends greatly on the goodwill of the employer. I personally have been very fortunate in this in one job, but felt very uncomfortable in another about having the odd day off. But even with a sympathetic employer, the pull between duty to the job and duty to one's child is enough to put one off working altogether. I would suggest that the only way round this is to have unpaid children's sick leave as a routine arrangement. This would of course have its difficulties, but where there is a great labour shortage it is better to have an employee some of the time rather than not at all. I don't think this would be abused, as it would only be necessary when a child was really ill — not for the odd cold, when a minder could cope.

Sickness and school holidays are the occasions when a mother's working life is most easily thrown off balance and again there are as many solutions as there are women working.

One must constantly bear in mind that whereas there may be many women who have tried and found the double life too difficult, all the women in this survey can manage to cope. And what is interesting about these women is that their *modus vivendi* does not cause so much strain that they are unable to continue. In all their answers about their children it becomes clear that as far as possible they let the needs of the children dictate their working patterns, and adjust when they have to. And in all their answers there is a lack of hysteria or guilt about their situations. The children's resentments and demands are set down alongside their pride and pleasure in their mothers' jobs, and none of the mothers seem to protest too much. The following are typical:

Freelance writer, B.B.C.: At the age of seven, when my son passed the door of my old office he was sorry, he said, not to see my name on the door! Yet I feel in many ways he would be happier if I did not have these outside interests. This is not because he is unhappy in any way, but naturally I cannot give him my *complete* attention, which he would like.

Teacher: My actual working times do not interfere with my children's timetable, except for that one lunch which the younger one is now used to, but still resents a bit. I do the preparation at the weekends when they can be with my husband, or in the evening. Of course their feelings are mixed, especially as I teach, but I think they get some benefit as I am more fully stretched, and therefore happier. We have been lucky in having very little illness to complicate matters.

G.P.: My children don't mind my working as long as it is not too frequently during the holidays and does not interfere with their social life. They don't like me to go to evening surgery more than once a week.

Publisher's reader: They aren't noticeably hostile, and seem to adapt well to it, though I feel that they'd like to have me at home all the time.

G.P.: . . . They certainly expect me to stay home if they are ill, and holidays present a real problem. They did not like me leaving to do blood donor sessions and leaving them with an au pair at home.

S.R.N.: My children aren't really perturbed by my working, except when extra hours are necessary in the present state of the hospital service, and routines are disturbed.

Advertising copywriter: They would prefer me to be at home—but the elder one is proud of my earning capacity, which I suppose is something.

Whereas many elaborate on the practical difficulties, almost no one mentions guilt. This is far removed from the theories of some years ago when convoluted expressions of guilt on the part of working mothers were the fashion. A novelist, who did not fill in a questionnaire, but instead sent a letter about the subject, spoke of this: 'I know when my first child was born, there was a fashionable theory that if a child was left without its mother in constant attendance it was bound to grow up delinquent. This was why I gave up a marvellous job I had been offered on a magazine. I think, now, it was a dotty belief, but it was a common one among women of my generation . . .'

And it is a belief that still has supporters, including the women in the survey who did not return to work until their children were in full-time schooling. The opposite viewpoint, that outside activity can contribute to the happiness of the child as well as the mother, is not new either. A Fabian comment in 1909 is not without relevance today: 'No one without long and constant experience among them can imagine the stultifying, paralysing effect on children in the first years of their life, of the mother whose activities are confined within the two or three-roomed houses of our great towns . . .'[7]

Between the extremes of constant attendance on the one hand and prolonged absence on the other, the part-time worker chooses a middle path.

She conscientiously employs the best help she can get to substitute for herself when her absence is unavoidable; but on the whole she arranges to be at home at crucial periods, like the beginning and end of the school day and at times of illness or for special events.

She would welcome more support in the shape of flexible nursery schools and aunt-type helpers.

She feels that her children gain on balance from her outside activities especially as they grow up; but she recognises an ambivalence in their attitude, too. Above all, she is pragmatic and adjusts her work schedule to suit their needs at different stages.

Her prime concern for the well-being of her children shows in every decision she makes and is the major reason for her preference for part-time work. She is convinced above all else that there is no substitute in their lives for herself.

6

HUSBANDS

Not surprisingly, the replies to the question about husbands' attitudes to their work are something like four times the length of those concerning their children. Husbands can more easily assert rights and lay down laws. Husbands are adult and articulate. Husbands, to a great extent, control the direction the family takes.

And in this sample it is quite clear that in the majority of cases husbands are glad that their wives are working, as well as being proud of them and encouraging them to do so.

One out of every two husbands filled in the relevant section in the questionnaire in his own hand. On the whole, they stressed their pleasure in a wife who is nourished by her own activity; one who does not have to depend on a vicarious share of her husband's life in the outside world. (In *The Captive Wife* a middle-class housewife describes the boredom of being home all day: 'He can share the housework as much as he likes, but he still walks out into a different world at half past nine every morning.')[8]

The husband of a medical artist, himself a timber agent, put it this way: 'Admiration predominates. My wife possesses exceptional organising ability, without which she could not possibly encompass her quite complex professional and family life. Beginners should abstain.' And the husband of a publisher, who is director of a group of trade magazines: 'She has to work—she would be frustrated if she did not. As she works only in the mornings—usually—she also gets lots of time with the children. This seems an ideal set-up for an intelligent mother, so I suppose she is very lucky. As for me, full-time housewives bore me.'

Pride and enthusiasm are in almost every instance the husbands' first response to the idea of their wives going to work; most of their answers indicate that the pleasing consequence, in terms of the marriage partnership, is a wife who is a more interesting and cheerful companion. 'I welcome my wife's having an outside interest of this kind,' says the director husband of a teacher. 'Undiluted domesticity is, I think, very confining and cramping.'

But within the context of their approval, the husbands enumerate the difficulties surrounding the work most realistically: inequitable pay, the sometimes unyielding problems of making suitable arrangement for domestic help or help with the children, the inadequate nursery facilities, and the difficulties of tax. Many of them feel that their wives, having been trained by society, have a responsibility to use this training. Even more than their wives they feel that society should make this easier for them. One also suspects that these men would not themselves tolerate anything like the conditions under which their wives work—especially when one remembers that the combination of outside work and duties at home sometimes makes a wife's working hours total as many as eighty a week.

A dietician's husband, himself a Customs and Excise officer, sums up the predominant attitude thus:

'I am very pleased that my wife has resumed her career. I think it is tragic that many intelligent women allow their brains to atrophy when they start to have children. My wife's job has made her life richer and more exhilarating. Nevertheless:

1. Childminding is complicated and wearing.
2. My wife's *net* income after working is disappointingly small.
3. The job should be a full-time one, and trying to do it on a part-time basis involves a lot of unpaid homework, which is bad for us both.

But on balance I am very keen for my wife to continue her career.'

The sum of all the practical objections is that if the burden becomes too much to carry, life at home is affected. This theme becomes a litany:

From wives:

'It is accepted as long as it does not interfere with running the home.'

'He approves so long as it does not seriously interfere with my care of the children.'

'He is glad I am working—as long as I do not suffer physically from exhaustion and so make family life difficult —but he realises I must do it.'

From husbands:

'I am entirely co-operative now that my wife confines her hours of work roughly to mine, and her present type of patients do not constantly phone in the evening. It was awful when she was a G.P. No evening and weekend was one's own.'

'I am all for it, so long as it doesn't make her too tired! Being myself in the position of trying to do two jobs I know the sort of strain involved—though I sometimes have to kick myself for not showing enough sympathy.'

As one reads through the questionnaires, one builds up a picture of domestic life in which, in the majority of cases, the husbands give what help they can in the home in operation. And where husband and wife are in the same the evenings and at weekends, in a spirit of friendly co-profession, there can be advantages in collaboration at home. 'I feel it very helpful that I can understand her work, and even lend a hand with the occasional reference,' says a psychologist. A novelist's husband, who is in B.B.C. administration, is helpful with proof-reading as well as with advice.

A medical editor writes: 'He has always been extremely co-operative and helpful about my working. We started married life as students together working for the same exams, and I think this helps.'

But if the husband is not of that temperament, or has

more work than he can manage, then it is a question of the wife somehow coping on her own, or giving up work. A social worker: 'As he has an extremely demanding job himself, he's unable to share extra burdens incurred by my work, and he would not want me to do more than is compatible with my responsibilities to the children and himself.' And a journalist: 'He is perfectly happy as long as my job doesn't entail frequent evening work. I think it important to be realistic about this; as long as the husband works, however, it is only natural that he should expect his meals cooked for him.'

The picture of domestic harmony is occasionally marred by small domestic irritations: the husband who writes, 'Where's my shirt?' And the theme that the wife's job is a 'hobby that pays for itself' and one that must be curtailed if it affects the smooth running of the home is often repeated. She is not, after all, the breadwinner: 'My attitude is motivated by the satisfaction my wife obtains from working rather than from the point of view of income,' writes a civil servant husband, married to an editor. And a doctor says of her husband: 'He is all for me working provided I don't take on too much, and provided, also, that I do not involve him—he is a very busy man—in a lot of inconvenience and domestic upheaval.' And again, the director husband of a teacher: 'She enjoys the work and the set-up is a convenient and reasonably adjustable one, and she isn't in it primarily for the money. So although I feel that the rate of payment is ludicrously low, and to that extent my wife is being exploited, I don't press the point—though I do register it now and again.'

This, then, is the predominant image: husbands who are in some cases a little indulgent or patronising about a part-time interest that pays its way, sometimes testy when the difficulties impinge on life at home, but on the whole helpful and encouraging in their wives' quest for a fuller life.

7

REWARDS AND DIFFICULTIES

Only five women in the whole sample say they would be happier not working. For the rest, there is positive pleasure gained out of putting education, training and experience to use. One answer, by a market research field investigator who has not found anything suitable to accord with her interests and experience, is worth quoting because it is indicative of what the women in this sample require of their work, and where the chief rewards lie:

'I have no profession, but very varied experience . . . insurance, banking . . . experience as a general clerk, then as a secretary to a Provident Fund . . . from which I was withdrawn to work as a statistician at the Board of Trade . . . worked as a publisher's assistant at the Royal Institute of International Affairs . . . after obtaining an insight into the retail side of the book trade at Harrods Bookshop became a partner in my own bookshop.

'I am now . . . bored, totally mindless . . . a widow with aged and dependent parents . . . I *can* only commit myself to work at short notice for short periods, and the work, though interesting socially, is not personally rewarding, as I am rather fidgeted by the end product . . . It is never very pleasing to work simply to have a few pounds extra without there being any meaning in the work . . .'

A teacher provides the other side of the coin. She is much happier since returning to work, which is 'the outlet' she needed, as she had not found life without work 'personally rewarding':

'I do not find housework and children frustrating, and I am, for example, a keen gardener. But I found suburban life unutterably boring—coffee, idle gossip, etc. I found I could never admit to my real interests, which are academic, and so to a certain extent I was forced to "live a lie".'

And a child psychotherapist states baldly: 'I could not conceive of a life without my work: a whole half of me would die.'

Barring a serious disruption, the women in this survey intend to go on working indefinitely. The standard inconveniences are all worth putting up with: income disproportionate to output of energy and talent, problems of domestic organisation, minor crises that can play havoc with important commitments; these and more are worth it in return for the personal satisfaction that work can afford.

Work feeds these women, providing nourishment of the quality Florence Nightingale described as essential a century ago: 'To have no food for our heads, no food for our hearts, no food for our activity, is that nothing? If we have no food for the body, how we do cry out . . .'[9]

One hundred years later the cry is still for food for head and heart: 'captive wives' have protested in recent years about their isolation, insecurity and loneliness. Only lately has a wider public become aware of an urgent need to ease the situation, to work out a deliberate scheme to integrate women in all their many roles into the structure of society.

There is no question that in all but a few instances the pleasure these women find in their work is whole-hearted, and that they have been happier since they began to work. They describe their rewards in terms of personal satisfaction in various ways:

Medical practitioner: I have a stimulating and interesting job. I get away from domestic chores, and am much fresher and better tempered to deal with the children etc. I like meeting people.

Educational psychologist: I am more *effective* in the house; less self-absorbed; more confident as a parent and citizen; better to look at and better company. One feels 'cut off' during the homebound years; unable to concentrate without immediate incentive. At least one can *sit down* at work; and only have to listen to one person at a time. Easier work than being a full-time mother.

Social worker: I certainly feel happier as I am using my training and feel more intellectually satisfied. In particular as my last child will very soon reach nursery school age and will be going after Christmas I feel that I will be a good deal better off than had I not worked outside the home.

Freelance T.V. and radio interviewer: For me it is very important to have an existence outside my home. The husband and children have shared the improvement. We all take it for granted now that I work.

Social worker: Despite all the difficulties of organisation involved I think that the family, the work, the community benefit. At least, I can only hope so.

Computer programmer: I am lazy when at home all day. Housework comes in fits and starts, but I would rather pay all I had to get that done and go out and use my brain, not my hands.

Clinical psychologist: I get much more positive pleasure in my home than I did when I was in it all the time. My husband and I always enjoy swopping bits of news in the evening and now I have a greater variety to offer.

Medical practitioner: I am immensely happier! To me it is the difference between being happy and unhappy. The regular work and the interest it brings every week and the need to read and learn is absolutely essential to me. It makes me enjoy my family and home much more than if I were completely tied to it.

Medical practitioner: I think, in general, a 'working Mum' is a more complete woman and makes a better mother and more useful one and certainly a more interesting partner for the husband. The standard of living is generally high because the working wife is a little fearful lest any fall in quality at home is blamed on her extra activity.

Only a few hedge this enthusiasm with reservations:

Psychoanalyst: I have always enjoyed having a professional life outside my home although when my children were young I would have preferred to have had an entirely domestic life if it had been possible.

Lecturer: At present I fluctuate between being fully domestic and being fed up with nothing but house and children; then I get a job and make arrangements for the children, the strains of this hectic life begin to tell and I long to return to domesticity, and I go through the whole cycle again.

Dental Surgeon: It is often very taxing when one comes home exhausted to have to cope with demanding children at bedtime.

Teacher: Much depends on the adequacy of my home help. There have been times, when I was depending on au pair girls, when I seriously thought of giving up outside work.

Legal adviser: I am undoubtedly happier—though possibly tireder.

The obstacles to going out to work are many and various. It is remarkable that none of the women in this survey have found them insuperable, although many others may have done so. The difficulties most often quoted (in decreasing order of importance) are: insufficient leave for sickness or children's holidays; lack of domestic help; income tax; surtax; lack of organised holiday activities for children; no promotion for part-time workers (although some part-timers do not seem to expect this); lack of flexible hours; distance from work; insecurity of tenure; lack of facilities for older dependents; cost of insurance contributions; age (especially women over forty); lack of nursery schools; cost of pension contributions.

A handful of women have not, surprisingly, encountered any of these difficulties. But the majority have had to cope with two or more of them.

Among the 250 women in the group, the difficulties encountered (in order of frequency of mention) are shown by the diagram below.

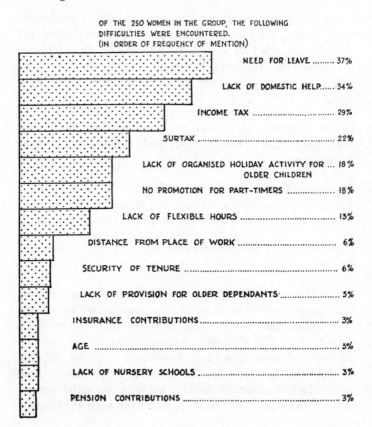

OF THE 250 WOMEN IN THE GROUP, THE FOLLOWING
DIFFICULTIES WERE ENCOUNTERED.
(IN ORDER OF FREQUENCY OF MENTION)

NEED FOR LEAVE 37%

LACK OF DOMESTIC HELP...... 34%

INCOME TAX 29%

SURTAX 22%

LACK OF ORGANISED HOLIDAY ACTIVITY FOR ... 18%
OLDER CHILDREN

NO PROMOTION FOR PART-TIMERS 18%

LACK OF FLEXIBLE HOURS 13%

DISTANCE FROM PLACE OF WORK 6%

SECURITY OF TENURE 6%

LACK OF PROVISION FOR OLDER DEPENDANTS 5%

INSURANCE CONTRIBUTIONS... 3%

AGE 3%

LACK OF NURSERY SCHOOLS 3%

PENSION CONTRIBUTIONS 3%

For most of these women time is more important than money. The need for maternity leave, and leave during school holidays and for illness, comes high on the list of priorities:

Editorial department of legal publishers: I need longer holidays, or absence for child's illness (without pay if necessary).

Market research field investigator: I am thankful for what I have, really. Society alone can help and it is slow to change. I wish I could obtain regular part-time work during term-time only.

Educational psychologist: I should certainly like to arrange to be at home during the children's holidays, and work longer in term.

Publisher's production manager: I need to cut the number of hours during school holidays. This can only be done by slowing down our production generally, which is what in fact happens.

G.P.: I would prefer not going to work during school holidays. I could then devote the time to family and to relations and friends who do not get entertained nearly as much as I should like and as they did before I went to work. One's social life—which is important—tends to suffer.

Library assistant: I need more leave in the summer holidays when temporary staff could be employed. Many library students and school leavers would like the experience and money.

Psychiatrist: I should like another two weeks' holiday a year to use for odd days—the day the children go back to boarding school, for instance. Odd days do not put one's colleagues out so much. One could work harder in term-time to make up for it.

Domiciliary midwife: I would like longer holidays with the children but feel it would be greedy.

Social worker: I would like to work 9.30-3.30 on three days a week during term time only.

Another social worker: Would work longer hours during school term and little, if at all, during holidays.

While yet another social worker offers a solution: Minimum to no work during school holdays . . . this could be managed by in-training of young postgraduates in administrative capacity and provision of full-time secretarial service.

Psychologist: I should like it accepted that one must have a week off before Christmas.

Computer programmer: I would arrange for maternity leave—this is not available in industry now, and each time I have a baby I have to resign and re-apply for employment later. And each time I have to re-negotiate with Accounts on tax codes, N.I. stamps, etc. I would like to work nearer home.

Even some teachers do not escape the leave problem.

Teacher: The children's holidays are a problem that has so far been managed with the help of grandmothers.

Next on the list of difficulties is domestic help. Below are a few comments in detail:

Medical practitioner: I could work more if I had some sort of educated housekeeper who could do most of the household planning for me, drive a car to fetch children from school etc., and yet have enough outside interest so as not to monopolise the children. I do not believe such a person exists.

Freelance editor and reader: If I could get it, I would have much more domestic help. Then I could work part-time in my employer's office, while my eldest child is at nursery school and the others are asleep. It would do them no harm.

Computer worker: I would like a contract for so many hours a week which would enable me to try for more regular domestic help or a nanny.

Medical practitioner: Increase amount of part-time work to ten hours per week and employ someone to help with the children regularly.

Musician: Make it possible to engage daily help for more than eight hours a week without being involved in a weekly stamp. Even ten hours a week would give me five days of two hours' help per day.

Freelance writer and broadcaster: I would have a *regular* part-time job which would fit in more easily with the domestic routine. Also I would like to find babyminding facilities which cost me only a small proportion of their cost now. Ideally, I would like tax relief on my payments for babyminding facilities and exemption from Selective Employment Tax.

Tax, income tax then surtax, comes next on the list of explicit difficulties. For example:

Historical researcher: The worst problem is paying surtax on money which goes to pay domestic help, especially in vitally needed professions like teaching and nursing.

Computer programmer: I would like to be assessed for tax as a single woman and allowed to set my expenses against tax.

Freelance writer and broadcaster: The basic problem financially is that I pay almost half my income on babyminding facilities and almost the other half on tax payable on my whole income. Tax relief on payments for domestic help and babyminding costs would solve this problem. Also perhaps relief from the National Insurance and Selective Employment Tax would be a great help. It could be said that I pay too much for babyminding but I would be very unhappy about leaving my child with a registered babyminder among a host of others.

One of the solutions offered for older children's holiday planning, another common difficulty, comes from an editor and publisher's reader: 'I have not yet had to face the holiday problem. I am taking five weeks off in the summer. Organised activities in the Christmas and Easter holidays would be a great help. There must be many part-time teachers who could take on some such scheme for the benefit of other professional women.'

Lack of promotion is discussed more fully in the next chapter.

.   .   .

The need for more flexible hours comes next in the catalogue of difficulties. For instance:

Neuropathologist: I would like to be at home from 4.30 to 7.30 and work from 8.30 a.m. to 4.30 p.m. But I am expected to be at hospital during the late afternoon.

Teacher: A more flexible timetable to enable me to take my son to and from nursery school, or have more nursery schools in my district, so that I wouldn't have to look so far afield as I do now.

S.R.N.: Reduce hours to about thirty a week and spend less time for meals on duty. (She works thirty-seven hours a week and this is considered part-time.)

Violin teacher: I should prefer not to teach during prayers so that I could start at 9.20, having washed up after breakfast. I should also prefer not to teach violins on Saturday mornings when the children need to shop, have haircuts, etc.

Medical practitioner: I would work regularly three mornings a week instead of one morning, one evening and on average at least one more variable half-day, as at present.

An occasional plea is made for more rigid scheduling:

Freelance T.V. interviewer: More planning in advance— so that I could know exactly when I shall be 'off duty' and when 'on'—also when I can take weekend breaks.

Distance from place of work is often a big problem for a variety of reasons:

Medical practitioner: I would like to find work nearer home—travelling forty-five minutes each way for three-and-a-half hours' work is a bit excessive.

Psychologist: I should like to work nearer home so that I could get back for lunch in the holidays.

Economist: No travelling during rush hours; working nearer home.

Security of tenure is a problem for many part-timers:

Freelance editor: I would try to find a job that was regular and not freelance. I suffer from never knowing how much I am going to earn and from not being able to regulate the inflow. Sometimes I have far too much to do at once.

Historical researcher: All these things present slight difficulties, but as my work is very flexible none is overwhelming. If the Civil Service Commission was to accept part-time workers on a permanent or semi-permanent basis, pensions and insurance, etc., would need negotiating.

Music teacher: As I am unqualified, I have a suspicion that if I make too much of a nuisance of myself, the education authorities may consider appointing one full-time peripatetic woodwind tutor for the whole area, to take over the teaching that is done at present by a man (also unqualified) who deals with clarinet, oboe, and some brass instruments, and myself. Though I am sure that, by now, the amount of teaching that the two of us get through in a week is well beyond one person's limit.

A number regretted the lack of useful and appropriate hours for nursery schools, and others wished for schools closer to home. A typical sigh comes from a school counsellor: 'Lack of useful proper hours for nursery schools. Two hours does not allow an afternoon's teaching without leaving the children to someone else's care.'

Problems imposed by place of work were not uncommon. On the one hand, for instance, a teaching coach writes: 'I should prefer to teach outside my home. At home there are too many distractions.' On the other hand another says: 'I would do more at home, though it is a good thing to go out and feel part of a bigger set-up.'

The problem of keeping in touch is mentioned by an architect, among others: 'Some way in which we could be kept up to date with the materials and forms of construction—very difficult for women at home just to sit and read magazines—there should be some form of publication aimed at them.'

There is more than one kind of housing problem, as an editor and publisher's reader points out: 'We need room in our flat for an au pair or other person who could look after the children. My problem is, therefore, ultimately one of housing.'

Although many cited that the care of elderly dependents presented difficulties, no solutions were offered; nor were the penalties imposed by insurance and pension contributions elaborated upon. It seems that these are on the whole accepted. While many difficulties are temporary or a way is found round them, some are part of life.

8

THE WORKING WORLD

'Most big companies have rules, and part-time work
makes things untidy.' —*Anonymous employer*.

Recently there was a rash of articles and television pro-
grammes whose chief theme—marking fifty years of women's
suffrage—was the frustration and complaint of housebound
women. From their tone it would seem that a new feminist
revival was in the air. *In Her Own Right*[10] spoke of 'the
need to secure recognition for the role women can play in
society,' as well as the rare 'good fortune of women who
manage to find jobs which stretch and challenge them.'

These are useful statements against which to set the
attitudes of the women in this survey. It is true to say that
most of them have little time to wonder whether their 'role'
is the most desirable one: they are playing things by ear,
taking what they find available or suitable in the way of
work, occasionally changing profession in order to achieve
this, and in a few instances even choosing, without noticeable regret, jobs that will not stretch and challenge them
too greatly—at least not while their children are young.

As Mrs. B.'s profile exemplified—and many others of the
questionnaires reinforce—the women in this group are
aware that times and situations change, and jobs may perhaps change with them.

From their replies it becomes clear that, contrary to the
popular notion that 'part-time' work is synonymous with
'low-calibre' work, most of these women feel that in their
present jobs their talents are being utilised to the full:
three quarters think that both their training and experience
are being put to full use.

The picture of their qualifications is shown in the diagram below.

OF THE 250 WOMEN IN THE GROUP:

40 % HAVE A DEGREE.

28 % HAVE A DIPLOMA.

28 % HAVE MORE THAN ONE QUALIFICATION.

4 % HAVE NO FORMAL QUALIFICATION.

Of those who do not think that they are making full use of their training and experience, some have deliberately chosen this alternative for the sake of having more time for their children:

G.P.: My previous training is more in obstetrics and blood transfusion, but the hours are impossible, and so I am working more generally, fortunate to have a job I can combine with children.

Teaching coach: I have now seven years' full-time teaching experience, but naturally with four children under school age it is impossible and certainly not desirable to do anything but an hour or two of teaching a week.

And some give other reasons. A computer programmer says: 'No, I am not making full use of my training. The reason is immobility on my part, and lack of opportunity.'

Quite a number say they are hampered by geography—living near their husband's work rather than their own.

Sometimes it is the fact of having to work part-time that excludes a woman from an interesting job:

Freelance writer: My experience and training are not

properly used, no. The B.B.C. does not employ producers part-time, nor does it employ administrators part-time. The only work I can get on a regular basis (even then only on short-term contract) is research, at half my previous rate of pay. I have also tried to get administrative jobs in local and central government, and in industry. Though I am suitably experienced, I could not get part-time jobs of this kind.

A minority, therefore, are not finding complete satisfaction in their jobs; but their tone on the whole is one of realistic regret rather than feminist complaint.

Journalist: My experience isn't fully used—I am not included enough in decision-making, simply because I do not come into the office on the days when policy conferences are held.

And a domiciliary midwife: My training isn't fully used—my work at the moment is mainly advising mothers with new babies. I am unable to be on call for patients in labour due to family commitments, and this I much regret.

It is interesting that very few of these women complain of the traditional bigotry and prejudice. On the whole, they adapt their skills in whatever way is feasible:

Occupational therapist: I have been unable to obtain work as an O.T. So I work as an unqualified nursery school teacher, which is what I am currently doing. I find that most of my acquired skills have not been used. Playing the piano is an asset—but that wasn't achieved by my training as an O.T.!

The emphasis on further training and refresher courses— seventy-six, or nearly a third of the total have undertaken some form of retraining—suggests that neither initiative nor ambition is lacking among women who prefer less than full-time work. (The details are in Appendix I.) Forty-five of the seventy-six paid for their own courses and thirty-one were sponsored. Many women in the sample have taken active steps to add to their qualifications or up-date themselves; by comparison very few have opted for a less demanding job than their training and experience warrant.

About one quarter of the sample have changed careers. Some have made a pragmatic adjustment to what work is available. But more have changed because in maturity they have discovered a change of interest or concern.

Twenty-seven women, including a number of former research workers, an administrative civil servant, a personnel manager, two physiotherapists and a film maker have become teachers, while fourteen, including a number of journalists and women working in industry, have taken up social work in some form. Several who have changed to teaching pointed out that they made the switch only for the sake of convenience, and are not making the best use of their talents.

OF THE 250 WOMEN IN THE GROUP, CAREERS CHANGED:

NOT AT ALL FOR 74%

TO TEACHING FOR................11%

TO SOCIAL WORK FOR........... 5%

TO OTHER CAREERS FOR........10%

Where a career has been interrupted (nearly everyone), a high proportion (nearly one-third) has returned to the same employer. This suggests that an employer is more likely to exercise flexibility vis-à-vis part-time work when the applicant is an individual already known. An advertising copywriter shows how this can happen, without any positive steps being taken: 'The firm I work for does not normally employ part-time copywriters, and would not deliberately undertake to do so. They were obliged to accept the situation because I had a baby and just didn't turn up full-time—yet I still managed to do the same work as I had before.'

There are many other comparable happenings:

Computer programmer: I am lucky as I have my job solely through long-time connections with my firm. I cannot believe that they would take on 'outside' part-timers.

Lecturer and coach: I did sixth form teaching where I had previously taught full-time before having my second child. It was my most successful part-time job, as I was already familiar with the staff and running of the school and this made it very easy for me to fit in.

Assistant editor: I worked for my present employers for about eighteen months before I had my first child, and took the job on the understanding that I would at least consider returning to work after having a child.

Freelance journalist and researcher: I worked for a research and intelligence unit for a short period full-time. Now I receive quite a lot of jobs from them that can be done at home.

Editorial assistant: I worked with the firm full-time until our first child was born, and have since continued working part-time at home.

But it is not always so easy:

Computer programmer: I tried my previous employer, and got an unco-operative response from the director though my departmental head had been encouraging.

Historical researcher: I wished to return to the Museum on

a part-time basis which would have been very suitable for
the cataloguing work for which I was qualified, but was not
allowed to do so. Part-time workers at the Assistant Keeper
level are not at all encouraged, although a few rare exceptions are made by individual heads of departments. Considering their bitter complaints when women leave to have a
family they should be much readier to make use of their
training on a part-time basis.

Occupational therapist: I made enquiries about working
at a certain hospital and found no specific arrangements
were known about the employment of married women with
young children, and that any agreements made about payment, part-time hours and holiday time off to correspond
with school holidays would have been highly unusual and
not encouraged.

Special arrangements for less than full-time work appear
in variety. The employees convey an overwhelming impres-
sion that the unusual terms they have been given have not
involved difficult adjustments for employers. They have
necessitated some initial change of attitude.

Computer programmer: I am down as a temporary employee—this is the only way in which the company can
employ me under their present rules.

Psychiatrist: The Region is allowing one full-time medical
Registrar job to be divided into two so that two married
women with families may do it. Eleven sessions are divided
into six and five, with the living-in hospital duties halved.
This is a new departure especially to draw in married
doctors.

Doctor: I work ten-elevenths of time and am allowed to
save up the part-time for long leave in the school holidays.
This is an excellent arrangement for me and was offered to

me by my employers in view of my family commitments.

Ante-natal teacher: I have arranged my own hours and conditions, but only because I am a pioneer in my field.

Publisher's production manager: I am the only member of his staff to work two days at the office and the rest of the time at home.

Educational psychologist: Everyone else in my particular clinic, apart from secretarial staff, is full-time. There is a certain amount of bureaucratic adjustment of holiday time calculated very finely by me as I am a precedent. In fact I certainly am meticulous about putting in more time than I need to.

The compensatory advantages to the employer for the concessions granted their employees far outweigh the drawbacks, according to most informants. Examples of gains accruing to the employer from the unusual employment contract are reason enough for a re-think of traditional policies.

School counsellor: I cram all my interviewing into one day, do case notes, phoning, research at home whereas if I were full-time I would fit all this in in work hours.

Social worker: I give many more hours than would be possible if the job was full-time. Two part-timers (as employed by my employer) are able to cover very much more ground, and between them attend many more functions than could be achieved by one person working alone.

Journalist: I work faster than the rest. I could not write more if I were present full-time, only share in more of the decisions and perks.

Teaching coach: No Selective Employment Tax. I do seven

hours, as do most others. This provides variety of stimulus for students and different qualifications.

And financial benefits to employers crop up:

Doctor: Employing me costs less than the equivalent share of a whole-time member of staff: no pension contribution, no desk or facilities other than a locker-cupboard.

Domiciliary midwife: No pension contributions. The fact that I am paid for the number of hours I do. Full-time people are paid forty hours a week regardless.

Lecturer: I do half the work of a full time colleague, man or woman, for approximately one-third of the salary. This is because of the hourly fee basis on which part-time lecturers are paid—they are treated as casuals! Part-timers are accepted in a limited sense, but I have so far not found any real acceptance of the part-time lecturer as a solid, permanent member of staff.

When examining their relationship with colleagues, the women in our survey found that, on the whole, full-time workers accepted them and eventually, if not always immediately, welcomed them. There are the obvious human limitations:

Copywriter: People are envious, I'm afraid, especially on hot summer days.

But in the great majority of cases the attitude reported is one of tolerance, helped by a little extra willingness and awareness by the part-timer.

Teacher: One sometimes has to lean heavily on their co-operative goodwill when one comes in infrequently. If one is co-operative and contributory in return all can run

smoothly, but not if one adopts a 'these-are-my-hours' attitude which other teachers can't possibly have.

And a Child Care Officer: Less than full-time workers are
not *usual* in my profession, but they are accepted . . . if the
individual is aware of difficulties other colleagues may en-
counter or have to carry on her behalf . . . It really does
depend so much on the attitude of the part-timers. I have
met little hostility—though sometimes one is helped by a
sense of humour. I feel you do need to prove your value
more than if you were full-time. You must be very willing
to offer *all* you can during the hours you are there.

As usual, it turns out to be a matter for the individuals
concerned. Another social worker: 'On the whole part-time
workers are accepted, and every consideration given to them
concerning their messages, or any crisis that may arise on
days they are not on duty. The full-time staff in my
particular work tend to be exceptionally helpful.' A lecturer describes her full-time colleagues as 'supportive . . .
the married ones understand my problems; the unmarried
ones would want to do the same as me themselves if they
marry.'

Doctors, teachers and social workers seem to be among
those most completely accepted by their professional colleagues. The reason for this is presumably that the work
load is heaviest in these understaffed occupations. They
stress both sharing of duties and teamwork.

Social worker: I think perhaps I may be particularly fortunate in working for a department and with colleagues who
are—by the very nature of their profession—intensely aware
of the stresses and strains of our particular work. Great
concern and interest is shown in the feelings of the workers
and the senior staff have provided a highly supportive back-
ground.

Not unnaturally, a few women report mixed feelings on

the part of colleagues. A copywriter speaks of 'acceptance but minor irritation when one is not available, but as long as one is on the end of a telephone this can be kept to a minimum.' And a child psychologist has found attitudes 'a little resentful, sometimes, in Clinics, if part-time therapists are doing too little and are not available for discussions, chores, etc.'

But the suggestion is frequently made that objections both by colleagues and employers are more often theoretical than real:

Research worker: One of the objections made to part-time workers in the Museum was that it would be considered to be unfair to the full-time staff who would have to bear the brunt of the day-to-day routine. This might be so, although the objections were theoretical only and I should have thought could be overcome.

Lecturer: Beneficial changes in *attitudes* would help, because one is looked on as being quite a different person from a full-time member of staff.

Librarian: In my own experience there was opposition in principle to the idea initially but in practice there has been complete co-operation. This may be due to my willingness to be flexible in my timetable and make up time I have lost through children's sickness etc.

Architect: I think there is a lot of scepticism about women architect-mothers returning to work. People feel that she won't be able to think of two things at once. It seems, however, that she does.

The part-timer can bring more to her job than the ability to think of two things at once. Time is so valuable to her that she is unlikely to waste it, a point made by many contributors.

Social worker: Other departments wonder how so much can be done. Perhaps we have the best of all worlds . . . though planning is required at home and in the office to accomplish this.

Does this copywriter state the case for part-timers too strongly? 'The terrible truth is that if everyone worked part-time the same amount of work would get done as now— or so I suspect. One spends less time in office gossip and reading the newspapers, calling unnecessary meetings and reading unnecessary memos.'

Part Two

A FEW PICTURES: UNPROCESSED

These particular questionnaires were chosen for their general interest, in order to let the readers see for themselves the individual pictures of activity that emerged from each set of answers. Beyond making sure that no two professions were duplicated, the deciding factor in the choice was the length and liveliness of the replies.

Questionnaire: Mrs. X.

SECTION A

1. *Present profession:* Social Work. (Assistant Secretary, Council of Social Service.)
2. *Previous profession(s):* Social Work.
3. *Professional qualifications:* Social Science Diploma.
4. *Age group:* 30-40.
5. *Marital status:* Married.
6. *Children at home:* One. Age 7.
7. *Husband's occupation:* Sales Executive.
8. *Paid domestic help:* Old age pensioner 4 hours per week. (Previous excellent help—also 4 hours per week—left at Christmas—not yet replaced.)
9. *Unpaid domestic help:* Invaluable Mother and Mother-in-law who come/take child when necessary.

SECTION B

10. *How many hours of work do you average in a week?*
    25. This does not include evening meetings—averaging

out at one per week—approx. three extra hours, including travelling time.

11. *How many weeks do you work in an average year?*
48.

12. *How does the weekly total compare with full-time colleagues?* More than half.

13. *When do you put in these hours?*
During school times, and evening meetings.

14. *Where do you do your work?*
In own locality.

15. *How would you describe your timetable?*
Flexible. Very.

SECTION C

16. *What is your pay (expressed as rate per hour)?*
10/-.

17. *Roughly what proportion of your earnings do you think remains after all your expenses have been deducted?*
Just over half.
Comments: Salary insufficient to employ living-in 'mother's help' and at same time achieve some financial gain. At present achieving financial advantage, but domestic situation unsatisfactory and a strain on personal resources. However, necessary to retain old age pensioner as domestic in order to cater for child emergencies. As yet I have not been fortunate enough to find supplementary help.

18. *Do you think your rate of pay is appropriate to the work you do?*
It is in keeping with scales of pay for social work—but these are very low!

19. *How does your rate of pay compare with that of full-time male colleagues?*
Equal.

20. *How does your rate of pay compare with that of full-time female colleagues?*
Equal.

SECTION D

21. *Do you think that full use is being made of:*
    your training? No.
    your experience? Yes.
22. *If not, why not?*
    Trained as a social worker. Now working mainly as administrator.
23. *Has your career been interrupted?*
    Yes.
24. *If so, for how long?*
    Five years.
25. *Have you returned to employers who previously employed you full-time?*
    No.
26. *Have you changed careers?* No.
    Why? Do not wish to—though frequently think of going into teaching in order to get school holidays free.
27. *Have you taken any form of further training to qualify you for your present job?*
    No.

SECTION E

28. *Do you belong to a professional Association?*
    No.

No answer to questions 29, 30, 31.

SECTION F

32. *Do you find that part-time workers are usual and accepted in your profession?*
    Not yet, though the necessity for them is gradually being realised. Profession not yet geared to necessary commitment of mothers with small children.
33. *Does your employer gain by employing you part-time?*
    Yes.
    e.g. through low overheads, no pension contributions, increased output, etc.

No pension contributions. Increased output.

Any others?

I give more hours than would be possible if job was full-time. Two part-timers (who are employed by my employer), are able to cover very much more ground and between them attend many more functions than could be achieved by one person working alone.

34. *Does your employer consider that you have been given unusual terms?*

No. Is extremely considerate.

35. *What is the attitude of your full-time colleagues to the engagement of part-time workers?*

In general they are so overworked that they are only too delighted to see an extra pair of hands—this means that part-time workers in their turn are overburdened and overworked.

36. *Do any of the following present special difficulty in the pursuit of your career?*

Lack of domestic help and lack of nursery schools.

Lack of organised holiday activity for older children.

Children's holidays. Whilst no complaint on salary, it is not sufficient to cover adequate household help and leave margin (see answer to 17) for household 'extras' etc. Some women must be in an untenable position if work is a necessity for them. Would it not be possible for at least a graded small allowance to be granted if one's salary is on the low side, say up to £1,000, if one has children under say 10, who should have *permanent living-in* figure (if mother works in school holidays)?

37. *What is your husband's attitude to your work?*

Agrees in principle that wives should have an occupation other than housekeeping. However the remuneration must provide for domestic help and even then leave something over; otherwise wife cannot be expected to cope with family, housekeeping and job reasonably dedicating sufficient time to each.

38. *What is your child's attitude to your work?*

Very interested. Somewhat proud yet resentful at times during school holidays, when looked after by grandmother. This is not altogether a satisfactory solution.

39. *If you were given a free hand what changes would you make in your working arrangements?*

Would work longer hours during school term, and little, if at all, during holidays.

40. *What changes would you suggest within your own profession to make the best possible use of trained professional part-time women?*

Flexibility as to hours. Realisation that more time off must be taken during school holidays. Provision of crêche or nursery school—perhaps by local authority—to cover children of professional parents. Provision of 'refresher courses'; and opportunities to re-specialise easily if desired. Courses would have to be in evenings.

41. *In your own personal experience, did anything turn up or develop that eased or improved your circumstances?*

Working with another part-timer with children. Both appreciate problems, help each other in emergencies.

42. *Would you like to return to full-time work?*

No—not until children are grown up.

43. *Have you yourself been happier with professional interests outside the home?*

Yes. Have infinitely more patience and understanding with my child and feel that our relationship has grown much stronger within last year. Fortunately have a generous and helpful husband, who puts up with washing at weekend etc.—which I personally abhor, but seem unable to prevent.

Questionnaire: Mrs. Y.

SECTION A

1. *Present profession:* Journalist.
2. *Previous profession(s):* Public Relations.

3. *Professional qualifications:* University degree in English. 10 years' experience in newspapers and magazines.
4. *Age group:* 30-40.
5. *Marital status:* Married.
6. *Children at home:* 3. Ages 14, 11, 3. (2 stepchildren.)
7. *Husband's occupation:* Scientific editor.
8. *Paid domestic help:* Mother's help; daily cleaner.
9. *Unpaid domestic help:* None.

SECTION B

10. *How many hours of work do you average in a week?*
20.
11. *How many weeks do you work in an average year?*
48.
12. *How does the weekly total compare with full-time colleagues?*
Half.
13. *When do you put in these hours?*
Tuesday, Wednesday, Thursday.
14. *Where do you do your work?*
Office; 9-2 p.m. Home Tuesday and Wednesday evenings.
15. *How would you describe your timetable?*
Flexible.

SECTION C

16. *What is your pay (expressed as rate per hour)?*
Approx. £1 10s. per hour.
17. *Roughly what proportion of your earnings do you think remains after all your expenses have been deducted?*
One third.
Comments: What hurts is the supertax my husband must pay. I would pay at least £5 a week for help, even if I didn't have my job (but I have subtracted it here as if it were an expense created by my job).

18. *Do you think your rate of pay is appropriate to the work you do?*
Yes.

19. *How does your rate of pay compare with that of full-time male colleagues?*
Equal. (More than young men, less than half of a senior male's pay.)

20. *How does your rate of pay compare with that of full-time female colleagues?*
Equal.

SECTION D

21. *Do you think that full use is being made of:*
   Your training? Yes.
   Your experience? No.

22. *If not, why not?*
I am not included enough in decision-making (because I do not come into the office on the days when policy conferences are held—Monday and Friday).

23. *Has your career been interrupted?*
Yes.

24. *If so, for how long?*
Two years.

25. *Have you returned to employers who previously employed you full-time?*
I worked for the same employer half-time ($3\frac{1}{2}$ days a week) before I had a baby.

26. *Have you changed careers?*
Only at the outset.
Why? I fell into journalism several years after University and found that it suited me admirably.

27. *Have you taken any form of further training to qualify you for your present job?*
A bit. Part-time.
Who paid for it?
I did.
Please describe the form it took.

Six months at the London School of Economics.

SECTION E

28. *Do you belong to a professional Association?*
No.

SECTION F

32. *Do you find that part-time workers are usual and accepted in your profession?*
Yes.

33. *Does your employer gain by employing you part-time?*
Yes . . . increased output. I work faster than the rest—
I could not write more if I were present full-time, only
share in more of the decisions and perks.

34. *Does your employer consider that you have been given unusual terms?*
Slightly.
Describe: I leave every day sharply at 2—when sometimes
it would be convenient if I were there in the late afternoon.

35. *What is the attitude of your full-time colleagues to the engagement of part-time workers?*
Friendly, but they tend to condescension.

36. *Do any of the following present special difficulty in the pursuit of your career?*
Surtax. Lack of organised holiday activity for older child-
ren. No promotion for part-time workers.

37. *What is your husband's attitude to your work?*
He encourages me, thinks that I should do more (and be
given more responsibility). He believes that women who
don't work are not interesting.

38. *What is your children's attitude to your work?*
They respect it. My step-children became more tractable
when it became clear that I was something more than a
housewife.

39. *If you were given a free hand what changes would you make in your own working arrangements?*

I would work for a publication which gave its writers by-lines, so that I could build a professional reputation despite my abbreviated working time.

40. *What changes would you suggest within your own profession to make the best possible use of trained professional part-time women?*

None—the jobs are there if women have the training before they have a family.

41. *In your own personal experience, did anything turn up or develop that eased or improved your circumstances?*

My job—the paper that I work for is enlightened and flexible.

42. *Would you like to return to full-time work?*

No.

43. *Have you yourself been happier with professional interests outside the home?*

Immeasurably.

Questionnaire: Mrs. Z.

SECTION A

1. *Present profession:* Housing management.
2. *Previous profession(s):* Same.
3. *Professional qualifications:* B.A. (Admin.) A.I.H.M.
4. *Age group:* 30-40.
5. *Marital status:* Married.
6. *Children at home:* 8 years. 6 years. 6 months.
7. *Husband's occupation:* Musician.
8. *Paid domestic help:* 1. Cleaner 2 hours per week.

      2. Care of baby one or two days.
Nappy service for six months.

9. *Unpaid domestic help:* Ironer (same person helps to clean). Baby sitters, and other friends.

SECTION B

10. *How many hours of work do you average in a week?*
10 hours.

11. *How many weeks do you work in an average year?*
   50. But any problems await my decision during holidays.
12. *How does the weekly total compare with full-time colleagues?*
   Less than half.
13. *When do you put in these hours?*
   One whole day or two halves and one or two evenings.
14. *Where do you do your work?*
   About 6 hours on the property per week, about 4 hours at home.
15. *How would you describe your timetable?*
   Adaptable at notice.

SECTION C

16. *What is your pay (expressed as rate per hour)?*
   15/- per hour.
17. *Roughly what proportion of your earnings do you think remains after all your expenses have been deducted?*
   Three quarters.
   Comments: Expenses increased with baby as she is not in group care as a toddler might be. Easily prepared food I tended to buy anyway. Some home dressmaking gets left undone and consequently a shop article has to be bought. I have to spend more on shoes for myself.
18. *Do you think your rate of pay is appropriate to the work you do?*
   Yes.
19. *How does your rate of pay compare with that of full-time male colleagues?*
   Equal.
20. *How does your rate of pay compare with that of full-time female colleagues?*
   Equal.

SECTION D

21. *Do you think that full use is being made of:*
   Your training? Yes.

Your experience? Yes.

23. *Has your career been interrupted?*

No. I was never dedicated to becoming a top manager with a borough and have always done as much housing as I wished.

24. *If so, for how long?*

Briefly—perhaps 2 years of just keeping in touch through meetings and articles.

25. *Have you returned to employers who previously employed you full-time?*

Not to municipal employer. As emergency help to a Housing Trust where I had been a student.

26. *Have you changed careers?*

No.

27. *Have you taken any form of further training to qualify you for your present job?*

No.

SECTION E

28. *Do you belong to a professional Association?*

Yes.

29. *If so, was your Association of help in obtaining your job?*

No.

30. *Does your Association take an interest in status and conditions of part-time workers?*

No—except I pay a lower membership rate by courtesy.

31. *What might your professional Association recommend to the profession and its employers in order to make the best possible use of trained professional part-time workers?*

Inclusion of part-time work on jobs list which should then go to any member who requested it. (Heads of offices are circularised and list pinned to board, but if member is not at work this does not help.)

SECTION F

32. *Do you find that part-time workers are usual and accepted in your profession?*
Not usual, but accepted in non-municipal offices. I have no experience of trying to get employment with a borough part-time.

33. *Does your employer gain by employing you part-time?*
Yes. Full-time cost would be £30 per week. I attend committee meetings gratis and spend some extra time on problem families who need help, advice, etc.

34. *Does your employer consider that you have been given unusual terms?*
No.

35. *What is the attitude of your full-time colleagues to the engagement of part-time workers?*
'I don't know how you do it!' and that it is a good thing —of course I have known them a long time and my qualifications are the same as theirs. I think they would mistrust unqualified entrants who weren't prepared to train and wanted manager jobs.

36. *Do any of the following present special difficulty in the pursuit of your career?*
Distance from work . . . Lack of nursery schools. Lack of organised holiday activity for older children: will be difficult probably—at the moment friends and sister help. Need for leave if children sick. Children's holidays. I have a very responsible position—plenty of big decisions. It would be impossible to become a top manager part-time. One has to be available all the time.

37. *What is your husband's attitude to your work?*
'Where's my shirt?'

38. *What is your children's attitude to your work?*
Mixed. When pre-school they don't always want to be away from Mum. Holidays: they are with friends and relatives and enjoy it without Mum. If worried I found it stopped if they were shown where one went and what one did.

39. *If you were given a free hand what changes would you make in your own working arrangements?*

There are no two weeks alike, the children vary everything all the time. From the employer's point of view it is left to me to do the work as I wish it to be done.

40. *What changes would you suggest within your own profession to make the best possible use of trained professional part-time women?*

I have worked for two London boroughs and I suspect Borough Housing Depts. could put part-timers to good use. Housing is very adaptable to this, especially where cases are passed to another office for completion. One or two blocks of flats could easily be managed part-time— but there aren't the people available.

41. *In your own personal experience, did anything turn up or develop that eased or improved your circumstances?*

Yes, there was a spate of new Housing Associations— three approached me for help. I only had time to help one. One finally had to employ a person full-time and the other still requires help if available (not near enough to me).

42. *Would you like to return to full-time work?*

Not at present. I might, if approached later, or if circumstances changed and I had to work full-time then I should certainly enjoy the work.

43. *Have you yourself been happier with professional interests outside the home?*

I believe one should keep involved with the profession one chooses and should earn the rate for the job. Other interests are not the same (they may be for some people of course)—involvement becomes essential in one's profession—it *makes* one think! I am on two local committees, one for Oxfam as Group Committee Treasurer and the other Family Study Play. But I think one should be able to earn one's living outside the house.

Part Three

SUMMING UP

> 'I think part-time work should be regarded as a normal part of a married woman's life and not merely a temporary substitute for full-time work while she rears her children.'
>
> *Questionnaire No. 302*

One of the most important and surprising pieces of information to have come out of this survey is that the majority of the women in it have no intention of returning to full-time work. Out of the 250, 215 answered the question, 'Would you like to return to full-time work?' with an emphatic 'no'.

Of the remaining thirty-five, many were extremely doubtful. They hedged round the thought of returning to work full-time with many conditions—'Only in the unlikely event of having a housekeeper,' for example; or, 'Well, I *might* consider it when my children are grown up. But even then, I'd like to have free time for what I want to do: community activities, for example,' or, 'Unless it was a family economic necessity, I wouldn't go back full time.'

According to a report published last year by the Department of Economic Affairs, a quarter of all women working in Britain do so on a part-time basis of some sort. It is very likely that many of them—the unqualified as well as the qualified—share the views of the women in this survey.

While considering the practical conclusions which emerge from their replies, it is essential to have in mind the flavour of these women's attitudes to full-time work: for it is this which must underline future thinking and planning concerning the employment of qualified married women.

Characteristic replies to the question: 'Would you like to return to full-time work?' emphasise the importance of the idea of less than full-time employment of married women as a permanent way of life.

'No!' writes the clinical psychologist. 'If the choice lay between full-time work and no work at all, I wouldn't work. Even with reasonable domestic help there is a lot I like to do in the home, and I would hate to miss school concerts, sports days, cricket matches, etc.'

'No,' writes a G.P. 'I feel I am gaining the maximum from work at present: a life of my own, purposeful contacts with others, and still I have time in the home and with the children.'

A speech therapist writes: 'I have never worked full-time. I do not feel I could do justice to my family if I did so and had, therefore, a permanent mother substitute—for in that case my children would be a type of luxury, to be embraced when weekends or holidays occurred! The only situation in which I would work full-time would be if I were widowed, and it was necessary for me to become the breadwinner.'

An economist: 'Pressure is being put on me at present to work full-time. But knowing I have at least one free day a week keeps me sane. It gives me a day to catch up on housework, see friends, or just be idle.'

An educationalist: 'Even when the children are older, and at full-time schooling, I think *nearly* full-time would be what I needed. Children need an elastic timetable—when a child needs one, through the odd ear-ache, say, one is torn in two. A mother is needed for such a short time that she should not have to feel criminal if she goes to work when a child is not well, and equally criminal if she stays at home.'

And a woodwind teacher: 'I wouldn't work again full-time. My children have got used to a full social life, with friends in to play and in for meals, as well as going to their friends. By the time the children are off our hands, my husband will be working towards retirement, and I should like to be free to spend some time with him.'

Leisure—to spend with children, husband and friends—is a precious commodity, desired and enjoyed by the middle-class wife. Yet shortages in the professions are increasing, and married women situated very like those in our survey will have to be recruited sooner or later. The means by which recruit and employer can be brought together are slowly being understood.

Acknowledgment of the value of part-time work is rare, but: 'The part-time woman worker,' said a recent *Times* editorial headed 'Waste of Skilled Women',[11] 'is just the person who could make an especially valuable contribution to solving staffing problems . . . The future of the National Health Service is gravely threatened by a shortage of doctors, yet while only three per cent of male doctors under the age of sixty-five are not engaged in medical work, the proportion of women is twenty-eight per cent. Obviously, a good number of these qualified women doctors would not wish to practise for family reasons, but there are many others who are deterred only by their inability to obtain suitable part-time appointments—especially in the hospital service. The education system, too, has failed to make proper provision for the potential supply of part-time women teachers.'

The first step towards bridging the gap, therefore, is to discover on what terms women in the medical and other professions will return to work.

Our findings suggest that any employer who wants to recruit such women will have to take into account the fact that the majority will choose to work less than full-time or not at all. Shortages are likely to persist or increase in professions where employers insist on recruitment of full-time workers, or even of part-time workers on too rigid a basis.

At the time of the 'Comeback' survey, it became clear that totally different attitudes prevailed among employers, even

in the same profession, emphasising yet again a factor that
has become a commonplace in this material: that it is an
attitude, or accident (which may or may not later be formalised into a policy), which initiates the possibility of part-
time work.

It is difficult enough for the mature woman who tries
to return to work on a *full-time* basis: the 'Comeback' group
found for example that while one bank professed to be
welcoming women of all ages, another could envisage no
possible use for mature women in its organisation. (The
banks they questioned were the 'Big Five' and Martins.)

'Employers like these,' wrote the 'Comeback' group in
1964—and their words still apply—'are ignoring the demographic changes amply illustrated in Professor Chester's
pioneering article "Growth, Productivity and Womanpower".'[12] Professor Chester divides employers into three
groups:

Firstly, '. . . those who blissfully ignore the demographic
changes and are able to convince themselves that this is
bound to be a passing phase. They would like to go on as
before, that is rely on a reserve army of devoted spinsters
as they were able to do in the inter-war years. Where difficulties are experienced in finding staff, there is often an
elaborate search for "hidden" causes . . . this is obviously
a forlorn hope.'

His second group consists of 'reactionaries'. They consider that a woman's sole place is in the home and link
working mothers with juvenile delinquency, although a
number of scientific surveys have in fact shown that there is
no causal relationship between the two.

The third group understands the demographic revolution
Professor Chester describes, and is adapting accordingly.
These employers—and there will have to be more of them
in the future—must rely increasingly on married and older
women, *working to some extent on their own terms,* if they
are to employ the same proportion of women to men as
previously, and meet ever-increasing shortages. 'Working on

their own terms' is another way of saying 'working less than full-time'. This is the burden of the argument of this book.

It is clear, then, that the employer must be prepared to make some modifications in his employment policy if he is to attract these women. But the information in the survey indicates that such modifications need not be complex, and that he would not be making an adaptation to his disadvantage.

One of the simplest arrangements—frequently referred to—is that the women simply arrive later and leave earlier than their colleagues—very often taking work home with them. 'An hour of concentrated work at home,' says a publisher's reader, 'is the equivalent of two hours strung out with less pressure in the office.' An administrator: 'If I were there all day I would do about the same amount of work as I do in half the time at home. It's simply that the pace of the office is much, much slower, and the distractions greater.' This arrangement of shorter hours in combination with work done at home is especially prevalent among architects, editors and copywriters in the survey. And the point is made several times that in any case the telephone brings the office to the home.

A number of suggestions are made relating to the re-arrangement of timetables. 'Less work in the school holidays in exchange for more term-time work,' is one which comes up frequently in different professions. This suggestion originates from inside the professions and is made by experienced women, who think that it is something which could be managed. It is evidently more practical than outsiders might imagine.

Teachers seek 'synchronised' or 'standardised' school holidays—though this also applies to mothers with children at different schools: state and private schools can vary by as much as three weeks in holiday span. A nursery school assistant, who says that in her own area education authorities are fairly accommodating towards part-time teachers, suggests that 'it would help if all schools had the same holidays

—they sometimes vary by a day or two, which can make things more difficult than they sound!' There are drawbacks inherent in not staggering in the holiday season of course— crowded roads and facilities. But the working woman's point of view has not yet been considered in this context.

Still on the subject of working hours, there is an increasing emphasis, both in medicine and welfare, on domiciliary work. Medical workers and others in sessional work suggest better relief systems, which would open up opportunities for sessional work. (Urgent shortages in casualty, anaesthetics and midwifery are singled out as amenable to simple reorganisation.) Other workers would simply like the 'occasional day off'.

Such changes would not only make life easier for those already in part-time work, but would open up opportunities for others by creating more posts, loosely described as 'part-time', which would be sufficiently adaptable for married women. The comment recurs that if employers used a little ingenuity and broke away from old habits, more part-time, otherwise termed 'flexible', work would become available.

'Pairing,' that is dividing the job between two or even more people, is another proposal frequently made; shift systems dividing the day or the week between two or more people, or operating on alternate weeks is a variant solution along similar lines. Occupations with severe staff shortages have already found this an eminently workable solution: the principal of St. Alban's High School and the matron of St. George's Hospital have expressed their enthusiasm in public.

In this connection, the inflexibility of local authorities, especially in the sphere of health and welfare, is so frequently criticised by participants in this survey that one must assume that local government is forfeiting the experience of many married women workers. It would seem that most local authorities and hospital boards prefer a vacancy and an overstrained service to making the adaptation that is needed to attract the married professional woman.

Another important aspect of the value of the part-timer to her employer is the relief of the work-load on full-time staff. The women in this survey have found that on the whole the full-time staff welcome them with friendliness and pleasure ('relieved' and 'grateful' are frequent descriptions). They tend to be understanding and co-operative in matters of detail and domestic commitment. The worst that one or two of the women have been dealt out from their full-time colleagues is condescension, and in rare cases they have found themselves the object of envy. Rather more express regret that contact with full-timers is sometimes slight and the part-time worker can feel 'out of it'. But, on the whole, staff relationships appear to be no problem and teamwork is far more common than isolation.

The implication that by allowing married women to work flexible hours employers are generously granting all the concessions is refuted consistently. The women in this survey repeat over and over again a number of special advantages to the employer, especially profit from the greater concentration and sense of urgency a woman brings to her work, and her reluctance to waste her time.

Employers are also getting a cash bargain in many cases: the savings in terms of desk and office space, in pension schemes, and, regrettably, in fewer increments than is normal with full-time promotions; these are mentioned frequently.

The fact that a third of the women in this inquiry have returned to employers for whom they originally worked full-time suggests that when the situation is neither anonymous nor theoretical a way is more easily found. The less tangible benefits that can accrue to the considerate employer are summed up by the journalist of Chapter 3: 'My paper has always made individual arrangements with its staff. This approach results in loyalty, and unstinting hard work when requested, because of the respect granted to individual attitudes towards the priorities of the family and the job.'

When an employer is faced with an unknown candidate,

policy often smothers the possibility of employment. This is the case with many local authorities, who could be among the largest, if not the largest, employers of part-time professional women. However, the most implacable institutions have bent on occasion to the single-minded energy and persistence of the applicant. This story of personal initiative, matched by a co-operative local authority, could be repeated many times to the benefit of all concerned. An economist writes:

'I wrote the briefest of notes to the City Treasurer, asking if there was any part-time work. I said I had a degree in Economics, and that my experience was in research and teaching—no more detail than that. I suggested that if he had nothing, he should pass my letter on to other departments.

'We met, discussed terms, and I was offered the job of part-time economist, to work with the one full-time economist—both new appointments. I asked for two days a week. (In theory I can do more in term-time and less during holidays, but this doesn't work out too well in practice, partly because I don't like to leave my two-year-old for more than two days a week.) I do whole days or half days, but they are strictly as for the rest of the staff—8.45 to 5.30. No nonsense about skipping out to buy some bacon, or leaving a bit early if a child needs collecting. I'm the only part-timer amongst the professionals, and the only woman, so I am very careful to conform to hours. On the other hand, if a Tuesday doesn't suit me one week, I can swap it for a Monday. And, of course, if I take a day off for a sick child, I have to make it up.

Economists are just beginning to be used by a few go-ahead local authorities (although the GLC has had hordes for some time). The fact that I got the job is due entirely to the Treasurer, who is a man who welcomes new ideas. He is particularly keen on cost-benefit analysis, which he wants to apply to the problems involved in expanding the city in the form of a new town. This is an enormous project for my boss alone, and he was glad of help.

'By pure chance there happened to be a course on cost-benefit analysis at the LSE last April (where, incidentally, I was the only woman among about forty men). Otherwise, we both learn as we go. We read a lot of the relevant literature. A lot depends on local knowledge and help from other departments, particularly the Planning Department with which we work very closely.

'. . . I love it. But as you see, it was luck . . .'

Presumably more women would go hard after jobs if they thought they had a chance of finding this kind of co-operation.

It seems likely too, that more women would seek out employment if their domestic circumstances changed. More organised activity for school-children's holidays would help as much as anything; high-calibre domestic workers (such as colleges of domestic science or nursery nursing might provide) would make the difference to many more.

It is clear, also, that more women would consider working if remuneration was better. While the women in this survey find the gains sufficient, there must be many more waiting for greater financial incentive, both in higher rates of pay and in fairer tax assessment. (These women more often criticise the Government for what it removes from the wage packet than the employer for perpetuating low salary scales.)

Most are finding the rewards adequate because they are in a privileged income group. Their privilege derives from their education and they share this advantage with their husbands.

Margaret Drabble has described her own comparative advantage, not dissimilar to that of many women in this survey, and the insuperable difficulties that stand in the way of many others who might wish to do likewise:

'I am tired of the debate myself, having won my own personal battle for the right to work by finding a job that fits in very well with my other commitments. But not all women are as lucky—very few women are as lucky—and it would be unfair to claim that their case no longer exists, simply because I no longer share it . . . Many professions are highly competitive, and require constant application: the years taken off for small children are a disqualification. Refresher courses in such careers as teaching, so constantly advertised as the ideal job for the working mother, are not nearly as widely available as they should be, and some of them, ludicrously enough, are residential, offering no accommodation for children. If one adds to such drawbacks the loss of confidence that very often accompanies the compulsory, if temporary, withdrawal from working life, one can see that it is extremely difficult for most women to resume employment after they have once given it up.'[13]

But it is more constructive to show what can be done than to dwell on what can't. In a period that has seen a revival of complaint about the 'captive wife', it is pleasant to be able to publish these success stories. Our informants have taught us a lot. They have effectively voiced their feeling that husbands and children profit as well as themselves from their contact with the working world. They have shown many different ways of managing two lives at once, have demonstrated how they manage, what they manage and what would enable them to manage more easily. Above all they have made the point that they don't want to manage full-time.

If 250 can succeed, then why not the thousands more who feel caught, trapped, demoralised, or who have made one or two attempts to get work and, having failed, have settled, for the moment, for an unsatisfying total domesticity.

The answer emerges strongly from this survey. Women are not likely to return to work until they can get better terms. In nearly every case this means shorter-than-average hours and a degree of flexibility in those hours, not only when the children are young, but right through their working life.

For in maturity women have normally become part of a network of community commitment; they carry unique social responsibilities, important among them family dependants, from elderly relations down to grandchildren. These commitments are necessary to a woman as an individual, and to society. They also demand a degree of flexibility and an invaluable capacity to improvise, virtues which all these women possess. Until outside organisations show at least some measure of this same flexibility, many qualified women are likely to stay at home. This is bound to happen eventually because shortages will dictate radical re-thinking. We should like to see it happen sooner rather than later.

A re-appraisal of the labour market is essential if married women are not to be wasted. The necessity for more flexibility is equally urgent for other sectors of the population. Denis Pym, the sociologist, said recently[14] that young people rate involvement higher than status, don't give a fig for security, and aren't interested in a professional life which offers hard work, promotion, tea-breaks and bonuses. He suggests that the bright and the young won't give their best in response to control imposed from above. 'All the time,' he said, 'British Governments are failing to develop and exploit the best characteristics they know the British to possess. The ideas of basic honesty and responsibility are ignored.' He uses a particular industrial complex as his example—but his point has application in most professions, where the work is individual, skilled, and involves the taking of responsibility: 'The people there have already integrated their work with their lives. They take work home and bring their leisure to the office. If they feel like knocking off for golf, they do.'

Pym is talking about the young. But he might well be describing any woman who has the capacity to work well in conditions which are 'adult', who has sufficient discipline to deliver what she is being paid for, and who has wide horizons and varied activities. Mrs. B.'s statement, 'my work came first before I had satisfactory personal relationships,' illustrates the general outlook. Women of the kind who answered this survey are not searching desperately for the material security of a job; they have experienced authority and responsibility in raising and running a family, and, in the process, have involved themselves in commitments to the community.

There are implications here for all women, not only for the comparatively privileged group represented in the survey.

If the pattern of less than full-time work becomes accepted as normal and even desirable because professional women press for it, and at the same time shortages hasten the process, other areas of employment may in turn become more open to flexible arrangements. The influence of a relatively small but vocal group may achieve changes in social policy to the ultimate benefit of all.

NOTES

p.17 [1] Ronald Bryden, *The Observer*, February 4, 1968.

p.18 [2] *Our Freedom and Its Results*, edited by Ray Strachey. Hogarth Press, 1936.

p.20 [3] F. le Gros Clark, *Women, Work and Age*. Nuffield Foundation, 1962.

p.20 [4] Dorothy Hodgkin quoted in *The Observer*, January 28, 1968.

p.24 [5] *ibid.*

p.48 [6] Since this time part relief on S.E.T. has been given to workers with a working week of less than 21 hours.

p.61 [7] *Fabian Women's Group,* edited by Mrs. Bernard Shaw, 1909.

p.62 [8] Hannah Gavron, *The Captive Wife*. Routledge, 1966.

p.67 [9] *Cassandra* by Florence Nightingale. Printed privately, 1852.

p.78. [10] *In Her Own Right*. Harrap, 1968.

p.106 [11] Third leader in *The Times*: 'Waste of Skilled Women', March 27, 1968.

p.107 [12] T. E. Chester, 'Growth, Productivity and Womanpower', in the *District Bank Review*, September 1962.

p.113 [13] Margaret Drabble, *The Listener*, April 4, 1968.

p.114 [14] Denis Pym in 'Why Bother to Work at All?' *The Observer*, February 11, 1968.

FURTHER TRAINING AND WHO PAID FOR IT

This list provides additional information about courses taken by the women in this survey in order to refresh or re-train. It is by no means a complete account of what is available, but may be of interest to some women considering returning to work themselves.

(Who paid for the training is in parenthesis.)

1. *MEDICAL*
A. *Sponsored courses.*

G.P.: Trainee-assistantship in general practice; obstetrical clinical assistantship in hospital (Ministry of Health).

G.P.: Postgraduate course (Ministry of Health).

G.P.: Postgraduate teaching course (Ministry of Health).

G.P.: Part-time family planning course (Family Planning Association).

G.P.: Full-time trainee fellowship in clinical and biochemical genetics. One year. (American National Institute of Public Health.)

Psychiatrist: Part-time lecture course (Regional Hospital Board).

B. *Paid by self.*

G.P.: One week's full-time refresher course every four years.

G.P.: Seminars with psychoanalyst for marital problem work.

G.P.: Full-time course of three months at Liverpool University, Certificate of Public Health.

G.P.: Eastman Dental Clinic: short course in dental anaesthetics.

G.P.: Family Planning Association course.

Psychiatrist: Four-year training at Institute of Psychoanalysis.

2. TEACHING
A. Sponsored courses.

Secondary school teacher: One-year postgraduate teaching diploma. Full-time. (Middlesex County Council.)

Teacher: Six-week refresher course. (Surrey Education Committee.)

Primary school teacher: Course for graduates, three weeks full-time, plus six weeks part-time. (A local Education Authority.)

Primary school teacher: Shortened two-year course. (A London Borough Education Department.)

Nursery school teacher: Course for infant teachers, evening classes at a University. (Local Education Authority.)

Tutor: Part-time university course in teacher training. (London County Council.)

Designer: Art school course. (Local Education Authority.)

Music teacher: Nine-day residential music course. (Somerset County Council.)

B. Paid by self.

School counsellor: Extra-mural diplomas.

Infant teacher: Refresher course one day a week for one term.

Art teacher: Evening classes.

Ballet teacher: Private study for ballet exams.

Art teacher: Pre-Diploma course at Regent St. Polytechnic.

Pottery teacher: Course at Richmond Institute of Further Education.

Music teacher: Private lessons and teacher's diploma course at Royal College of Music.

Teachers (several): Evening classes.

3. SOCIAL WORK
A. Sponsored courses.

Medical social worker: One-week full-time intensive refresher course. (Group Hospital Management Committee, Staines.)

Medical social worker: One-week full-time intensive refresher course. (Regional Hospital Board.)

Medical social worker: Diplomas in Social Studies and Applied Social Studies. (Ministry of Health.)

Child care officer: One-month intensive re-entry course. (London County Council.)

Social caseworker: One-year course of weekly lectures. (Surrey County Council.)

Psychiatric social worker: Full-time one-year course at London School of Economics. (Local Education Authority.)

B. Paid by self.

Social caseworker: Extra-mural university course.

Social caseworker: Diploma course, London School of Economics.

Social caseworker: Evening classes.

Citizens' Advice Bureau organiser: Evening classes (and lectures sponsored by Council of Social Service).

Child care officer: Weekend courses plus seminars and lectures.

Medical social worker: Seminars and lectures.

Medical social worker: One week's intensive refresher course.

4. OTHER TRAINING
A. Sponsored courses.

Computer programmers: Normal full-time training courses: 1 day-3 weeks (Employers). Evening classes (Employers).

Ante-natal teacher: Weekend courses (National Childbirth Trust).

Domiciliary midwife: One week's residential course (Lambeth Borough Council).

Dietician: One-week refresher course (King Edward VII Fund for Hospitals).

Social psychologist: Three-year Ph.D. course (Medical Research Council).

Clinical psychologist: One-week course (Medical Research Council).

B. Paid by self.

Orthoptist: Three-day refresher course.
Barrister: Lectures at Law Tutors.

USEFUL ADDRESSES

Part-time Employment Agencies

The University Women's Part-Time Employment Agency,
49 Lyonsdown Ave, New Barnet, Herts. Tel.: 01-449-2525.
Organiser: Mrs. A. R. Bradford. (London area.)

Freelance Work for Women,
91 Parkway, London N.W.1. Tel.: 01-485-9527.
Director: Mrs. Joan Wilkens.

Graduaid,
14 Blackford Avenue, Edinburgh 9. Tel.: Newington 1164.
Organiser: Mrs. I. Ewen. (Scotland)

The Graduate Women's Part-Time Employment Bureau,
2 Wilderness Court, Onslow Village, Guildford, Surrey.
Tel.: Guildford 5403.
Organiser: Mrs. T. Hunt. (Surrey)

Service Unlimited (Southern),
62A The Hundred, Romsey, Hants. Tel.: Romsey 3643.
Organiser: Mrs. P. R. Ackroyd. (Southern Counties)

Service Unlimited (Westward),
Rivendell, Dyer's Lane, Iron Acton, Bristol.
Tel.: Rangeworthy 358.
Organiser: Mrs. J. Wyton. (Bristol & South-West)

West Riding University Women's Part-Time Employment
    Agency,
26 Hall Rise, Burley-in-Wharfedale, Ilkley, Yorks.
Tel.: Burley-in-Wharfedale 3145.

Organiser: Mrs. A. Lomax.
also Mrs. J. Wilson, 21 Southway, Eldwick, Bingley, Yorks.
Tel.: Bingley 4228. (West Riding)

The Anglian Agency for Part-Time Employment,
25 Greenbanks, Melbourn, Royston, Herts.
Tel.: Melbourn 784.
Organiser: Mrs. A. McCallum. (East Anglia & Cambs.)

The North-West Part-Time Employment Agency,
39 Balmoral Avenue, Whitefield, Lancs.
Tel.: Whitefield 3819.
Organiser: Mrs. M. Beer.
also Miss A. Cohen, 8 Overbrook Drive, Prestwick.
    (Manchester area)

The University Women's Part-Time Employment Agency:
    South Wales.
35 St. Ina Road, Heath, Cardiff. Tel.: Cardiff 60129.
Organiser: Mrs. B. Michalovich. (South Wales)

The University Women's Part-Time Employment Agency:
    North West Region,
46 Downham Road North, Heswall, Cheshire.
Tel.: Heswall 5087.
Organiser: Mrs. B. Jones. (Liverpool & Cheshire)

New Horizons Employment Agency (for married women
    with degrees and other professional qualifications),
6 Ridgemount, Oaklands Drive, Weybridge, Surrey.
Tel.: Walton-on-Thames 40189.
Organiser: Mrs. L. Taylor. (N.-E. Surrey & West of London)

Nottingham.
7 Varden Avenue, Lenton Abbey, Nottingham. NG9 2SJ.
Tel.: Nottingham 258816.
Organiser: Mrs. R. Smith.

Glasgow.
56a Partickhill Road, Glasgow 1. Tel.: not yet known.
Organiser: Mrs. S. Turnbull.

The Midlands Part-Time Employment Agency,
39 Prospect Lane, Solihull, Warwicks. Tel.: Shirley 5730.
Organiser: Mrs. B. M. Chapple. (Midlands)

Teamwork,
28 Courthope Road, London N.W.3. Tel.: 01-485-1950.
Organiser: Mrs. Pickering.
also Mrs. Ahrends. Tel.: 01-485-7570.

The Oxford Women's Part-Time Agency,
33 Moorbank, Blackbird Leys, Oxford. Tel.: Oxford 79855.
   (Oxford)

Women's Employment Federation (advice only),
251 Brompton Road, London S.W.3. Tel.: KEN 9237.

Women's Information & Study Centre,
3 Queen's Ride, London S.W.13. Tel.: 01-788-3040.

The Probus Agency (part-time employment for professional
   and business women),
20 Kelvinside Gardens, Glasgow N.W. Tel.: Maryhill 2538.
Organisers: Mrs. S. Norton and Mrs. S. Turnbull.

ROOM FOR IMPROVEMENT

Recommendations for action arising from this survey.

I. The creation of more part-time posts
   in schools: morning and afternoon teachers, specialist appointments.
   in medical fields: establishment of domiciliary teams, more health centres; more ancilliary help for general practitioners; hospital rescheduling for medical auxiliaries as well as nurses; shared surgeries.
   in social work: pairing or twinning in child care, school welfare, casework, administration.
   in office work: recognition that the telephone can be an office extension and much work can be accomplished at home.
   in field work: appointments can often be made outside 'normal' hours and this type of work lends itself especially well to part-time work.
   in institutional work: library and museum work can often be sessional; Institutional care would benefit from more rota work.

II. The introduction of re-training or refresher courses planned for married women, non-residential and not competitive with school leavers and young graduates. Hours geared to requirements of school-children.

III. Higher rewards and more responsibility for less than full-time work in recognition that this type of work will become increasingly sought by highly qualified women whose talents would otherwise be wasted.
   Reforms are needed urgently:
   1. Better rates of pay as the gap between what women earn and what they pay out is narrowing. (Financial incentives are lacking where they are most needed, *vide* nursing.)

2. Separate and less punitive assessment of tax, including relief for domestic help and from Selective Employment Tax in essential employment.

3. Permanent tenure and opportunities for promotion which are too frequently denied the less than full-time employee at the moment.

4. Access to help in secretarial and other ancillary work that does not demand a woman's skill but only her time.

IV. Introduction of greater flexibility into working hours for married women:

Work loads can often be concentrated into term time. A simple shortening of the working day can meet her needs in some cases with no commensurate loss of productivity.

Increased reliance on rotas can cover unexpected illnesses.

Greater use of temporary staff (students and trainees) in holidays.

V. Provision of facilities for child care:

Crêches and nursery schools at hospitals and local authority offices as well as at schools for part-time workers.

Recruitment corps of domestic workers trained in child care, with priority for professional mothers. Also children's nurses for temporary work with sick children at home.

Establishment of holiday camps for older children.

VI. Centralised information and recruitment services:

Professional bodies should keep registers and advertise part-time posts. (Very few women declared that their Professional Associations had helped them to find their jobs, and few said that their Associations were interested in the part-time worker. Exceptions: the Architectural Association; The Medical Women's Federation.) The part-timer is on her own when it comes to job hunting and seeking her terms of employment.

Ministry of Labour should provide vocational guidance and registers. (The Ministry of Labour keeps a

Professional and Executive Register for full-time work only. A spokesman says, 'There is no part-time register because all the notifications we receive are for full-time work.' There is no person on the staff of the Register with special responsibilities for women.)